Human Resource Management

Essential Perspectives

Second Edition

Robert L. Mathis

University of Nebraska at Omaha

John H. Jackson

University of Wyoming

SOUTH-WESTERN

THOMSON LEARNING

Australia · Canada · Mexico · Singapore · Spain · United Kingdom · United States

Human Resource Management: Essential Perspectives, 2/e, by Robert L. Mathis and John H. Jackson

Vice President/Publisher: Dave Shaut
Senior Acquisitions Editor: Charles McCormick, Jr.
Developmental Editor: Mardell Toomey
Marketing Manager: Joe Sabatino
Production Editor: Margaret M. Bril
Manufacturing Coordinator: Sandee Milewski
Media Technology Editor: Diane van Bakel
Media Production Editor: Robin Browning
Cover Design: Jennifer Lambert/Jen2 Design
Cover Photo: ©2001 PhotoDisc, Inc.
Production House: WordCrafters Editorial Services, Inc.
Compositor: WordCrafters Editorial Services, Inc.
Printer: Webcom Limited

Printed in Canada
1 2 3 4 5   04 03 02 01

For more information contact South-Western, 5101 Madison Road, Cincinnati, Ohio, 45227 or find us on the Internet at http://www.swcollege.com

For permission to use material from this text or product, contact us by
• **telephone: 1-800-730-2214**
• **fax: 1-800-730-2215**
• **web:** http://www.thomsonrights.com

Library of Congress Cataloging-in-Publication Data
Human resource management : essential perspectives / Robert L. Mathis, John H. Jackson, [authors].—2nd ed.
   p. cm.
   Includes bibliographical references and index.
   ISBN 0-324-10758-7
      1. Personnel management. I. Mathis, Robert., 1944– II. Jackson, John Harold.
HF5549.H7854 2001
658.3—dc21

                                                                              00-067076

About the Authors

DR. ROBERT L. MATHIS

Dr. Robert Mathis is a Professor of Management at the University of Nebraska at Omaha (UNO). Born and raised in Texas, he received a BBA and MBA from Texas Tech University and a Ph.D. in management and organization from the University of Colorado. At UNO he has received the university's "Excellence in Teaching" award.

Dr. Mathis has co-authored several books and has published numerous articles covering a variety of topics over the last twenty-five years. On the professional level, Dr. Mathis has held numerous national offices in the Society for Human Resource Management and in other professional organizations, including the Academy of Management. He also has served as President of the Human Resource Certification Institute (HRCI) and is certified as a Senior Professional in Human Resources (SPHR) by HRCI.

He has had extensive consulting experiences with organizations of all sizes in a variety of areas. Firms assisted have been in telecommunications, telemarketing, financial, manufacturing, retail, health care, and utility industries. He has extensive specialized consulting experience in establishing or revising compensation plans for small and medium-sized firms. Internationally, Dr. Mathis has consulting and training experience with organizations in Australia, Lithuania, Romania, Moldova, and Taiwan.

DR. JOHN H. JACKSON

Dr. John H. Jackson is a Professor of Management at the University of Wyoming. Born in Alaska, he received his BBA and MBA from Texas Tech University. He then worked in the telecommunications industry in human resources management for several years. After leaving that industry, he completed his doctoral studies at the University of Colorado and received his Ph.D. in management and organization.

During his academic career, Dr. Jackson has authored four other college texts and more than fifty articles and papers, including those appearing in *Academy of Management Review, Journal of Management, Human Resources Management,* and *Human Resource Planning.* He has consulted widely with a variety of organizations on HR and management development matters and has served as an expert witness in a number of HR-related cases.

At the University of Wyoming he served two terms as department head in the Department of Management and Marketing. Dr. Jackson has received teaching awards and worked with two-way interactive television for MBA students. He designed one of the first classes in the nation on Business, Environment, and Natural Resources. In addition to teaching, Dr. Jackson is President of Silverwood Ranches, Inc.

Preface

The importance of HR issues for managers and organizations is evident every day. As indicated by frequent headlines and news media reports on downsizing, workforce shortages, sexual harassment, union activity, and other topics, the management of human resources is growing in impact throughout the United States and the world. Many individuals are affected by HR issues; consequently, they will benefit by becoming more knowledgeable about HR management. Those interested in the field of HR management must know more about the nature of various HR activities. Every manager's HR actions can have major consequences for organizations. This book has been prepared to provide an overview of HR management for students, HR practitioners, and others in organizations.

A need exists for a moderately priced overview of HR management that both HR practitioners and students can use. The positive reception of the first edition of *Human Resource Management: Essential Perspectives* proved this. Consequently, we are pleased to provide an updated version. In addition, this book presents information in a way that makes sense to various industry groups and professional organizations. Finally, this condensed view of HR management also addresses the tremendous interest in U.S. practices of HR management in other countries, making it a valuable resource for managers worldwide.

As authors, it is our belief that this book will be a useful and interesting resource for those desiring an overview of the important issues and practices in HR management. It is our hope that this book will contribute to more effective management of human resources in organizations.

Robert L. Mathis, Ph.D., SPHR
John H. Jackson, Ph.D.

Table of Contents

CHAPTER THREE   *Equal Employment Opportunity* 35

CHAPTER 1

Strategic Human Resource Management and Planning

Human resources can and should play an integral role in the strategic management of an organization. Human resources are increasingly seen as having the potential to create competitive advantage for an organization.

The people in an organization can provide a competitive advantage. Throughout the book, it will be emphasized that the people as human resources may contribute to and affect the competitive success of the organization. **Human resource (HR) management** deals with the design of formal systems in an organization to ensure the effective and efficient use of human talent to accomplish organizational goals.

HR MANAGEMENT CHALLENGES

The environment faced by HR management is a challenging one because changes are occurring rapidly across a wide range of issues. A study by the Hudson Institute, entitled *Workforce 2020*, has highlighted some of the more important workforce issues that are identified in the following sections.[1]

Economic and Technological Change

Several economic changes have altered employment and occupational patterns in the United States. A major change is the shift of jobs from manufacturing and agriculture to service industries and telecommunications. This shift has meant that some organizations have had to reduce the number of employees, while

1

others have had to attract and retain employees with different capabilities than previously were needed.

Occupational Shifts

Projections of the growth and decline in jobs illustrate the economic and employment shifts currently occurring. It is interesting to note that most of the fastest-growing occupations percentagewise are related to information technology or health care. The increase in technology jobs is due to the rapid increase in the use of information technology, such as databases, system design and analysis, and desktop publishing. The health-care jobs are growing as a result of the aging of the U.S. population and workforce, a factor discussed later. Due to the increased use of information technology, global linkages are now more extensive, resulting in production and transportation being coordinated worldwide. Loss of manufacturing jobs in the United States has been replaced with jobs in information technology, financial services, health care, and retail services. In summary, the U.S. economy is becoming a service economy, and that shift is expected to continue. More than 80% of U.S. jobs are in service industries, and most new jobs created by 2006 also will be in services. It is estimated that manufacturing jobs will represent only 12 to 15% of all U.S. jobs by that date.[2]

Workforce Availability and Quality

In many parts of the United States today, significant workforce shortages exist due to an inadequate supply of workers with the skills needed to perform the jobs being added. In the last several years news reports have regularly described tight labor markets, with unemployment rates in some locales below 3%. Also, industries and companies continually report shortages of qualified, experienced workers. Today *contingent workers* (temporary workers, independent contractors, leased employees, and part-timers) represent more than 20% of the workforce. Many employers operate with a core group of regular employees with critical skills, and then expand and contract the workforce through the use of contingent workers. This practice requires determining staffing needs and deciding in advance which employees and positions should form the core group and which should be more fluid.

Demographics and Diversity

The U.S. workforce has been changing dramatically. It is more diverse racially, women are in the labor force in much greater numbers than ever before, and the average age of the workforce is now considerably older than before. As a result of these demographic shifts, HR management in organizations has had to adapt to this more varied labor force both externally and internally. Projections by the U.S. Bureau of Labor Statistics are that the racial/ethnic mix of the U.S. workforce will continue to shift. The white labor force is expected to decline from 80% of the workforce in 1986 to about 73% by 2006. It is projected that by 2020, about 20% of the U.S. population will be age 65 or older, and that there will be as many people over age 65 as there will be ages 20–35. The aging of the population also is reflected in the occupational shifts noted previously. The growth in medically related jobs will be due primarily to providing care to older people, who will live longer and need greater medical care. Taken together, these aging issues mean that HR professionals will continue to face significant staffing difficulties. Efforts to attract older workers through the use of part-time and flexible staffing will increase.[3] Also, as more older workers with a lifetime of experience and skills retire, HR will face significant challenges in replacing them with workers who have similar capabilities and work ethic.

Balancing Work and Family

For many workers in the United States, balancing the demands of family and work is a significant challenge. While this balancing has always been a concern, the growth in the number of working women and dual-career couples has resulted in greater tensions for many workers. To respond to these concerns, many employers are facing pressures to provide "family-friendly" policies and benefits. The assistance given by employers ranges from maintaining references on child-care providers to establishing on-site child-care and elder-care facilities. Also, according to the Family and Medical Leave Act employers with at least fifty workers must provide up to twelve weeks of unpaid parental/family leave.

Organizational Restructuring

Many organizations have restructured in the past few years in order to become more competitive. As part of the organizational changes, many organizations have "rightsized" by either (1) eliminating layers of managers, (2) closing facilities, (3) merging with other organizations, or (4) outplacing workers. A common transformation has been to flatten organizations by removing several layers of management and to improve productivity, quality, and service while also reducing costs. As a result, jobs are redesigned and people affected. One of the challenges that HR management faces with organizational restructuring is dealing with the human consequences of such change.

HR MANAGEMENT ACTIVITIES

The central focus for HR management must be on contributing to organizational success. As Figure 1-1 depicts, HR management usually is composed of several groups of interlinked activities. However, the performance of these HR activities is done in the context of a specific organization, which is represented by the inner rings in Figure 1-1. All managers with HR responsibilities must consider external environmental forces—such as legal, political, economic, social, cultural, and technological ones—when addressing HR activities.

FIGURE 1-1 Management Activities

HR Planning and Analysis

HR planning and analysis activities have several facets. Through *HR planning,* managers attempt to anticipate forces that will influence the future supply of and demand for employees. Having a *human resource information system (HRIS)* to provide accurate and timely information for HR planning is crucial.

⚹Equal Employment Opportunity

Compliance with equal employment opportunity (EEO) laws and regulations affects all other HR activities. For instance, strategic HR plans must ensure availability of a *diversity* of individuals to meet *affirmative action* requirements. In addition, when recruiting, selecting, and training individuals, all managers must be aware of EEO requirements.

Staffing

The aim of staffing is to provide an adequate supply of qualified individuals to fill the jobs in an organization. By studying what workers do, *job analysis* provides the foundation for the staffing function. From this, *job descriptions* and *job specifications* can be prepared and used to *recruit* applicants for job openings. The *selection process* is then concerned with choosing the most qualified individuals to fill jobs in the organization.

HR Development

Beginning with the *orientation* of new employees, HR training and development also includes *job-skill training.* As jobs evolve and change, ongoing *retraining* is necessary to accommodate technological changes. Encouraging *development* of all employees, including supervisors and managers, is necessary to prepare organizations for future challenges. *Career planning* identifies paths and activities for individual employees as they develop within the organization. Assessing how employees perform their jobs and make improvements is the focus of *performance management.*

Compensation and Benefits

Compensation rewards people for performing organizational work through *pay, incentives,* and *benefits.* Employers must develop and refine their basic *wage* and *salary* systems. Also, *incentive programs* such as gainsharing are growing in usage. The rapid increase in the costs of benefits, especially health-care benefits, will continue to be a major issue.

Health, Safety, and Security

The physical and mental health and safety of employees are vital concerns. The traditional concern for *safety* has focused on eliminating accidents and injuries at work. Additional concerns are *health* issues arising from hazardous work with certain chemicals and newer technologies. Also, workplace *security* has grown in importance, in response to the increasing number of acts of workplace violence.

Employee and Labor-Management Relations

The relationship between managers and their employees must be handled effectively if both the employees and the organization are to prosper together. Whether or not the employees are represented by a union, employee rights must be addressed. It is important to develop, communicate, and update HR policies and rules so that managers and employees alike know what is expected.

NATURE OF HR MANAGEMENT

The field of HR management is undergoing transition because organizations themselves are changing. As a result, the terminology in the field is in transition. Traditionally called *personnel departments,* many of these entities have been renamed *human resource departments.*

HR as Employee Advocate

Traditionally, HR has been viewed as the "employee advocate" in organizations. As HR management has changed, it has become clear that there is a need for HR to balance being the advocate for employees and being a business contributor. This balancing means that it is vital for HR professionals to represent employee issues and concerns in the organization. However, just being an effective employee advocate is not sufficient. Instead, HR professionals must be strategic contributors, partners with operating managers, administratively efficient, and cost effective.

Roles of HR Management

As Figure 1-2 depicts, HR management may play three roles in organizations. The traditional administrative and operational roles of HR management have broadened to include more strategic elements. It should be emphasized that as HR roles shift to the right of Figure 1-2, the previous roles still must be met and the additional ones performed. Also, the continuum shows that as it becomes more strategic, the primary focus of HR considers longer time horizons and the broader impact of HR decisions.

The administrative role of HR management is heavily oriented to processing and keeping employee records. Maintaining employee files and HR-related

FIGURE 1-2   HR Management Roles

	ADMINISTRATIVE	OPERATIONAL	STRATEGIC
Focus	Administrative processing and record keeping	Operational support	Organization-wide, global
Timing	Short term (less than 1 year)	Intermediate term (1–2 years)	Longer term (2–5 years)
Typical Activities	• Administering employee benefits • Conducting new employee orientations • Interpreting HR policies and procedures • Preparing equal employment reports	• Managing compensation programs • Recruiting and selecting for current openings • Conducting safety training • Resolving employee complaints	• Assessing workforce trends and issues • Engaging in community workforce development planning • Assisting in organizational restructuring and downsizing • Advising on mergers or acquisitions • Planning compensation strategies

databases, processing employee benefits claims, answering questions about tuition and/or sick leave policies, and compiling and submitting required state and federal government reports are all examples of the administrative nature of HR management. These activities must be performed efficiently and promptly.

Typically, the operational role of HR management requires HR professionals to identify and implement operational programs and policies in the organization. They must carry out the HR portion of strategic plans developed by top management.

One of the most important shifts in the emphasis of HR management in the past few years has been the recognition of HR as a strategic business contributor. Even organizations that are not-for-profit, such as governmental or social service entities, must manage human resources in an advantageous manner. Based upon the research and writings of a number of HR scholars, including David Ulrich of the University of Michigan, the importance of HR as a *strategic business partner* has been stressed.[4] This emphasis involves HR in several areas:

▶ Involvement in strategic planning
▶ Decision making on mergers, acquisitions, and downsizing
▶ Redesigning organizations and work processes
▶ Ensuring financial accountability for HR results
▶ Attracting and retaining human resources
▶ Developing human resource capabilities
▶ Identifying and rewarding performance

Ethics and HR Management

As the issues faced by HR managers have increased in number and complexity, so have the pressures and challenges of acting ethically. Ethical issues pose fundamental questions about fairness, justice, truthfulness, and social responsibility. Concerns have been raised about the ethical standards used by managers and employees, particularly those in business organizations.

For the HR manager, there are ethical ways in which the manager ought to act relative to a given human resource issue. However, determining ethical actions is not always easy. Just complying with the laws does not guarantee ethical behavior. Laws and regulations cannot cover every situation that HR professionals and employees will face. Instead, people must be guided by values and personal behavior "codes."

HR Management Competencies and Careers

Changes in the HR field are leading to changes in the competencies and capabilities of individuals in HR management. The development of broader competencies by HR professionals will ensure that HR management plays a strategic role in organizational success. One study found that HR professionals must have core competencies, level-specific competencies, and role-specific competencies.[5] Based on these and other studies and surveys, it appears that three sets of capabilities are important for HR professionals:

▶ Knowledge of business and organization
▶ Influence and change management
▶ Knowledge about specific HR activities

One of the characteristics of a professional field is having a means to certify the knowledge and competence of members of the profession. The most well-known certification program for HR generalists is administered by the Human Resource Certification Institute (HRCI), which is affiliated with the Society for Human Resource Management (SHRM). The body of knowledge of the HR field, as used by HRCI, is contained in Appendix A. This outline reveals the breadth and depth of knowledge necessary for HR professionals. Additionally, those who want to succeed in the field must update their knowledge continually. Reading the literature listed in Appendix C is one way to do this. A listing of major HR-related associations and organizations is contained in Appendix B.

ORGANIZATIONAL STRATEGIES AND HR PLANNING

Strategic planning must include planning for the people necessary to carry out the organizational strategic plan. The competitive organizational strategy of the firm becomes the basis for **human resource (HR) planning**, which is the process of analyzing and identifying the need for and availability of human resources.

FIGURE 1-3   HR Planning Process

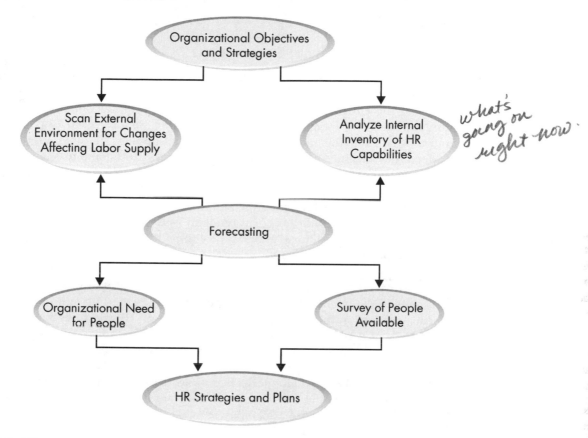

This section discusses HR planning responsibilities, the importance of HR planning in small and entrepreneurial organizations, and the HR planning process.

The steps in the HR planning process are shown in Figure 1-3. Notice that the HR planning process begins with considering the organizational objectives and strategies. Then both external and internal assessments of HR needs and supply sources must be done and forecasts developed. Key to assessing internal human resources is having information accessible through a human resource information system (HRIS). Once the assessments are complete, mismatches between HR supply and HR demand must be identified. HR strategies and plans to address the imbalance, both short and long term, must be developed.

HR strategies are the means used to aid the organization in managing the supply and demand for human resources. These HR strategies provide overall direction for how HR activities will be developed and managed. Finally, specific HR plans are developed to provide more specific direction for the management of HR activities.

Scanning the External Environment

At the heart of strategic planning is the knowledge gained from scanning the external environment for changes. **Environmental scanning** is the process of studying the environment of the organization to pinpoint opportunities and threats. Scanning especially affects HR planning because each organization must draw from the same labor market that supplies all other employers. Indeed, one measure of organizational effectiveness is the ability of an organization to compete for a sufficient supply of human resources with the appropriate capabilities.

Many factors can influence the supply of labor available to an employer. Some of the more significant environmental factors include government influences, economic conditions, geographic competitive concerns, and workforce composition and work patterns.

Government Influences. A major element that affects labor supply is the government. Today, managers are confronted with an expanding and often bewildering array of government rules as regulation of HR activities has steadily increased. As a result, HR planning must be done by individuals who understand the legal requirements of various government regulations.

Economic Conditions. The general business cycle of recessions and booms also affects HR planning. Such factors as interest rates, inflation, and economic growth help determine the availability of workers and figure into organizational plans and objectives. Decisions on wages, overtime, and hiring or laying off workers all hinge on economic conditions.

Geographic and Competitive Concerns. Employers must consider the following geographic and competitive concerns in making HR plans:

▶ Net migration into the area
▶ Other employers in the area
▶ Employee resistance to geographic relocation
▶ Direct competitors in the area
▶ Impact of international competition on the area

Workforce Composition and Work Patterns. Changes in the composition of the workforce, combined with the use of varied work patterns, have created workplaces and organizations that are very different from those of a decade ago. The traditional work schedule, in which employees work full time, eight hours a day, five days a week at the employer's place of operations, is in transition. Organizations have been experimenting with many different possibilities for change: the four-day, forty-hour week; the four-day, thirty-two-hour week; the three-day week; and flexible scheduling. Many employers have adopted some flexibility in work schedules and locations. Changes of this nature must be considered in HR planning. Also, a growing number of employers are allowing workers to use widely different working arrangements. Some employees work partly at home and partly at an office, and share office space with other "office nomads." *Telecommuting* is the process of going to work via electronic computing and telecommunications equipment.

Other employees have *virtual offices,* which means that their offices are wherever they are, whenever they are there. An office could be a customer's project room, an airport conference room, a work suite in a hotel resort, a business-class seat on an international airline flight, or even a rental car. The shift to such arrangements means that work is done anywhere, anytime, and that people are judged more on results than on "putting in time." Greater trust, less direct supervision, and more self-scheduling are all job characteristics of those with virtual offices and other less traditional arrangements.

Internal Assessment of Organizational Workforce

Analyzing the jobs that will need to be done and the skills of people currently available to do them is the next part of HR planning. The needs of the organization must be compared against the labor supply available. The starting point for evaluating internal strengths and weaknesses is an audit of the jobs currently being done in the organization. The following questions are addressed during the internal assessment:

- What jobs now exist? *- get a list of all jobs in Company*
- How many individuals are performing each job? *-*
- What are the reporting relationships of jobs? *- who do they Report to*
- How essential is each job? *- what would happen if job was eliminated*
- What jobs will be needed to implement the organizational strategy?
- What are the characteristics of anticipated jobs?

Organizational Capabilities Inventory. As those doing HR planning gain an understanding of current jobs and the new jobs that will be necessary to carry out organizational plans, they can prepare an "inventory" of current employees and their capabilities. The basic source of data on employees is the HR records in the organization. By using different databases in an HRIS, HR planners can identify the employees' capabilities, knowledges, and skills and then use these inventories to determine long-range needs for recruiting, selection, and HR development.

Human Resource Information Systems *- Data Base Program*

Computers have simplified the task of analyzing vast amounts of data, and they can be invaluable aids in HR management, from payroll processing to record retention. With computer hardware, software, and databases, organizations can keep records and information better, as well as retrieve data more easily.

A **human resource information system (HRIS)** is an integrated system designed to provide information used in HR decision making. An HRIS has many uses in an organization. The most basic is the automation of payroll and benefit activities. With an HRIS, employees' time records are entered into the system, and the appropriate deductions and other individual adjustments are reflected in the final paychecks. As a result of HRIS development and implementation in many organizations, several payroll functions are being transferred from accounting departments to HR departments. Another common use of HRIS is EEO/affirmative action tracking.

An HRIS and the Internet. The dramatic increase in the use of the Internet is raising possibilities and concerns for HR professionals, particularly when establishing an HRIS. Use of Web-based information systems has allowed the firm's HR unit to become more administratively efficient and to be able to deal with more strategic and longer-term HR planning issues.

Ensuring Security and Privacy. Two other issues of concern are *security* and *privacy*. Controls must be built into the system to restrict indiscriminate access to HRIS data on employees. For instance, health insurance claims might identify someone who has undergone psychiatric counseling or treatment for alcoholism, and access to such information must be limited. Likewise, performance appraisal ratings on employees must be guarded.

Forecasting

The information gathered from external environmental scanning and assessment of internal strengths and weaknesses is used to predict or forecast HR supply and demand in light of organizational objectives and strategies. **Forecasting** uses information from the past and present to identify expected future conditions. Of course, projections for the future are subject to error. Changes in the conditions on which the projections are based might even completely invalidate them, which is the chance forecasters take. Usually, though, experienced people are able to forecast with enough accuracy to benefit organizational long-range planning.

Approaches to forecasting human resources range from a manager's best guess to a rigorous and complex computer simulation of the labor force. Simple assumptions may be sufficient in certain instances, but complex models may be necessary for others. It is beyond the scope of this text to discuss in detail the numerous methods of forecasting available.

HR forecasting should be done over three planning periods: *short range,* *intermediate,* and *long range.* The most commonly used planning period is short range, usually a period of six months to one year. This level of planning is routine in many organizations because very few assumptions about the future are necessary for such short-range plans. The main emphasis in HR forecasting to date has been on forecasting organizational need for human resources, or HR demand. The demand for employees can be calculated on an organization-wide basis and/or calculated based on the needs of individual units in the organization.

Forecasting human resources can be done using two frameworks. One approach considers specific openings that are likely to occur and uses that information as the basis for planning. The openings (or demands) are created when employees leave positions because of promotions, transfers, and terminations. The analysis always begins with the top positions in the organization, because from those there can be no promotions to a higher level.

Once the need for human resources has been forecasted, then their availability or supply must be identified. Forecasting the availability of human resources considers both external and internal supplies. The external supply of potential employees available to the organization needs to be estimated. Here are some of the factors that may be considered:

- ▶ Net migration into and out of the area
- ▶ Individuals entering and leaving the workforce
- ▶ Individuals graduating from schools and colleges
- ▶ Economic forecasts for the next few years
- ▶ Technological developments and shifts

MANAGING A HUMAN RESOURCE SURPLUS

All efforts involved in HR planning will be futile unless management takes action to implement the plans. Managerial actions vary depending on whether a surplus or a shortage of workers has been forecast. But regardless of the means, the actions are difficult because they require that some employees be removed from the organization and workforce reductions are necessary.

Workforce Reductions and the WARN Act

The Worker Adjustment and Retraining Notification (WARN) Act requires employers to give sixty days' notice before a layoff or facility closing involving more than fifty people. However, part-time employees working fewer than twenty hours per week do not count toward the fifty employees. Also, seasonal employees do not have to receive WARN notification. The WARN Act imposes stiff fines on employers who do not follow the required process and give proper notice.

Downsizing

During the past decade in the United States, a large number of firms initiated aggressive programs to downsize their workforces. **Downsizing** is reducing the size of an organizational workforce. To avoid the negative terminology, some firms have called it "rightsizing." But the result is that many people lose their jobs.

Consequences of Downsizing. Despite the extensive usage of downsizing throughout many industries and organizations, there are significant questions about the longer-term value of downsizing. In some companies, organizational performance has not improved significantly, although operating expenses decline in the short term. What these firms and others have found is that just cutting payroll expenses does not produce profits and strengthen growth if the firm's products, services, and productivity are flawed. In some downsizings, so many employees in critical areas have been eliminated—or have chosen to leave—that customer service and productivity have declined. Just as critical is the impact of job elimination on the remaining employees. One survey found that in 69% of the surveyed firms, employee morale declined in the short term; 28% of the firms had longer-term declines in employee morale. Additionally, resignations and employee turnover all increased substantially in the year following the downsizing.[6] These consequences are crucial challenges to be addressed by HR management when organizational restructurings occur.

Managing Survivors of Downsizing. A common myth is that those who are still around after downsizing in any of its many forms are so glad to have jobs that they pose no problems to the organization. However, some observers draw an analogy between those who survive downsizing and those who survive wartime but experience guilt because they were spared while their friends were not. The result is that the performance of the survivors and the communications throughout the organization may be affected.[7]

Downsizing has inspired various innovative ways of removing people from the payroll, sometimes on a massive scale. Several alternatives can be used when downsizing must occur; attrition and hiring freezes, early retirement buyouts, and layoffs are the most common.

Attrition and Hiring Freezes. *Attrition* occurs when individuals who quit, die, or retire are not replaced. With this approach, no one is cut out of a job, but those who remain must handle the same workload with fewer people. Unless turnover is high, attrition will eliminate only a relatively small number of employees. Therefore, employers may use a method that combines attrition with a *hiring freeze*. This method is usually received with better employee understanding than many of the other methods.

Early Retirement Buyouts. *Early retirement* is a means of encouraging senior workers to leave the organization early. As an incentive, employers make additional payments to employees so that they will not be penalized economically until their pensions and Social Security benefits take effect. Such voluntary termination programs, or buyouts, may entice employees to quit with financial incentives. They are widely viewed as ways to accomplish workforce reduction without resorting to layoffs and individual firings.

Layoffs. *Layoffs* occur when employees are put on unpaid leaves of absence. If business improves for the employer, then employees can be called back to work. Layoffs may be an appropriate downsizing strategy if there is a temporary downturn in an industry. Nevertheless, careful planning of layoffs is essential.

may be called back [handwritten margin note]

Outplacement Services. **Outplacement** is a group of services provided to displaced employees to give them support and assistance. It is most often used with those involuntarily removed because of performance problems or elimination of jobs. A variety of services may be available to displaced employees. Outplacement services typically include personal career counseling, résumé preparation and typing services, interviewing workshops, and referral assistance. Such services are generally provided by outside firms that specialize in outplacement assistance.

NOTES

1. Richard W. Judy and Carol D'Amico, *Workforce 2020: Work and Workers in the 21st Century* (Indianapolis, IN: Hudson Institute, 1997).
2. U.S. Department of Labor, Bureau of Labor Statistics, 2001.
3. Rick Garnitz, "Aging Workforce Poses an HR Challenge," *ACA News,* March 1999, 20–21; and Carol Patton, "Golden Solutions," *Human Resource Executive,* August 1998, 63–65.
4. Dave Ulrich, *Human Resource Champions* (Boston: Harvard Business School Press, 1997).
5. Stephen C. Schoonover, *HR Competencies for the Year 2000* (Alexandria, VA: SHRM Foundation, 1998).
6. American Management Association, "Corporate Job Creation, Job Elimination, and Downsizing," 1997 Survey, 1–8.
7. Alex M. Susskind, Vernon D. Miller, and J. David Johnson, "Downsizing and Structural Holes," *Communication Research* 25, 1998, 30–65.

SUGGESTED READINGS

Ken Dychtwald, *Age Power,* Tarcher Publishing, 1999.

John McCarter and Ray Schreyer, *The Best 100 Web Sites for HR Professionals,* Impact Publications, 2000.

Towers Perrin, *Making Mergers Work: The Strategic Importance of People,* SHRM Foundation, 2000.

Robert K. Prescott, William J. Rothwell, and Maria W. Taylor, *The Strategic Human Resource Leader,* Davies-Black Publishing, 1998.

SUGGESTED INTERNET RESOURCES

SHRM Online. Contains wide-ranging information on HR issues and trends from the Society for Human Resource Management.
http://www.shrm.org

International Personnel Management Association. Provides information primarily on governmental and public-sector HR management.
http://www.ipma-hr.org

2

Organizational Performance and Global Effectiveness

People are key to enhancing organizational performance. The effectiveness of HR management practices can impact both organizational and global productivity.

The kinds of HR systems and practices that organizations develop differ to some extent. They evolve in response to different circumstances, but it is becoming clear that HR management does affect organizational effectiveness and the ability to compete. Individuals are valuable as resources for the managers who rely on them to accomplish work. In some organizations the people and the innovative ideas they generate are really the "product" that the firm produces. In others, depending on the job design, people may be a necessary but much smaller part of the overall effort, because machines do most of the work.

ORGANIZATIONAL AND GLOBAL PRODUCTIVITY

The more productive an organization, the better its competitive advantage because its costs to produce a unit of output are lower. Better productivity does not necessarily mean more is produced; perhaps fewer people (or less money or time) were used to produce the same amount. A useful way to measure the productivity of a workforce is the total cost of people per unit of output. In its most basic sense, **productivity** is a measure of the quantity and quality of work done, considering the cost of the resources it took to do the work. It is also useful to view productivity as a ratio between organizational input and output. This ratio indicates the value added by an organization or in an economy.

•

Global Competitiveness and Productivity

At the national level, productivity is of concern for several reasons. First, high productivity leads to higher standards of living, as shown by the greater ability of a country to pay for what its citizens want. Next, increases in national wage levels (the cost of paying employees) without increases in national productivity lead to inflation, which results in an increase in costs and a decrease in purchasing power. Finally, lower rates of productivity make for higher labor costs and a less competitive position for a nation's products in the world marketplace.

Organizations and Productivity

Productivity at the organizational level ultimately affects profitability and competitiveness in a for-profit organization and total costs in a not-for-profit organization. Decisions made about the value of an organization often are based on its productivity.

Perhaps the resources used for productivity in organizations most closely scrutinized are human resources. Many of the activities undertaken in an HR system deal with individual or organizational productivity. Pay, appraisal systems, training, selection, job design, and compensation are HR activities concerned very directly with productivity.[1]

Increasing Productivity

U.S. firms have made significant efforts to improve organizational productivity. Many productivity improvement efforts have focused on the workforce. The early stages included downsizing, reengineering jobs, increasing computer usage, and working employees harder. These approaches have done as much good as possible in some firms. Some ideas for the next step in productivity improvement include the following:

▶ Outsourcing
▶ Making workers more efficient with capital equipment
▶ Replacing workers with equipment
▶ Helping workers work better
▶ Redesigning the work

Quality and Productivity

Quality of production also must be considered part of productivity, because one alternative might be to produce more, but at a lower quality. At one time, American goods suffered as a result of this trade-off. W. Edwards Deming, an American quality expert, argued that getting the job done right the *first time*—through pride in craftsmanship, excellent training, and an unwillingness to tolerate delays, defects, and mistakes—is important to quality production.

Service

Delivering high-quality customer service is another important outcome that affects organizational competitive performance. High quality and productivity are both important in the final aspect of performance considered here—*customer service*. Such service begins with product design and includes interaction with customers, which hopefully results in meeting of customers' needs. Some firms do not produce products, only services. The U.S. economy is estimated to be composed of more than 80% service jobs, including retail, banking, travel, and government, where service is the basis for competition. Service excellence is difficult to define, but people know it when they see it. In many organizations, service quality is affected significantly by the individual employees who interact with customers.

INDIVIDUAL/ORGANIZATIONAL RELATIONSHIPS

At one time loyalty and long service with one company were considered an appropriate individual/organizational relationship. Recently, changes have been noted in both loyalty and length of service, with employees leaving more frequently. Several factors are driving the changes, including the following:

- ▶ Mergers and acquisitions
- ▶ Self-employment and contingent work
- ▶ Outsourcing jobs
- ▶ Loss of employment security
- ▶ Less management job tenure
- ▶ Altered psychological contracts

The Psychological Contract

The long-term economic health of most organizations depends on the efforts of employees with the appropriate knowledge, skills, and abilities. One concept that has been useful in discussing employees' relationships with the organization is that of a **psychological contract**, which refers to the unwritten expectations that employees and employers have about the nature of their work relationships. Because the psychological contract is individual and subjective in nature, it focuses on expectations about "fairness" that may not be defined clearly by employees.

The transformation in the psychological contract mirrors an evolution in which organizations have moved from employing individuals who perform tasks, to employing individuals expected to produce results. Rather than just paying them to follow orders and put in time, increasingly employers are expecting employees to use their skills and capabilities to accomplish organizational results. Studies suggest that employees *do* believe in these unwritten agreements

FIGURE 2-1   Model of Individual/Organizational Performance

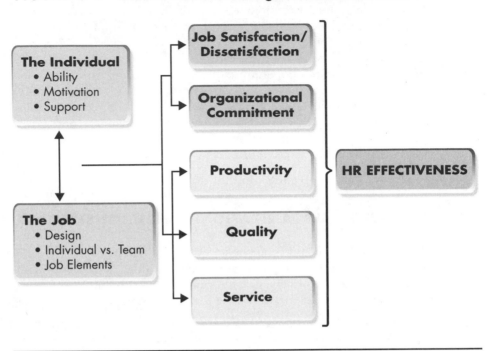

or psychological contracts, and hope their employers will keep their side of the agreement. When employers do not, employees feel a minimal need to contribute to organizational productivity because they no longer trust employers. Thus, employees' loyalty has been affected negatively. Sometimes loyalty is necessary, and it can be successfully based on a new psychological contract with the following expectations:

Employers provide	**Employees contribute**
► Competitive compensation	► Continuous performance improvement
► Benefits tailored to the workforce	► Reasonable tenure with the organizattion
► Flexibility to balance work and home life	► Extra effort when needed

The conceptual model shown in Figure 2-1 shows the linkages, beginning with individual and job characteristics, that lead to job satisfaction, organizational commitment, and affect the organizational outcomes—productivity, quality, and service—already discussed.

PRODUCTIVITY AND JOB DESIGN

Job design refers to organizing tasks, duties, and responsibilities into a productive unit of work. It involves job content and the effect of jobs on employees. Identifying the components of a given job is an integral part of job design.

Job design can influence *performance* in certain jobs, especially those where employee motivation can make a substantial difference. Lower costs through reduced turnover and absenteeism also are related to good job design. Also, job design can affect *job satisfaction*. Because people are more satisfied with certain job configurations than with others, it is important to be able to identify what makes a "good" job.

The person/job fit is a simple but important concept that involves matching characteristics of people with characteristics of jobs. Obviously, if a person does not fit a job, either the person can be changed or replaced, or the job can be altered. In the past, it was much more common to make the round person fit the square job. However, successfully "reshaping" people is not easy to do. By redesigning jobs, the person/job fit can be improved more easily. Jobs may be designed properly when they are first established or "reengineered" later.

Consequences of Job Design

Jobs designed to take advantage of these important job characteristics are more likely to be positively received by employees. Such characteristics help distinguish between "good" and "bad" jobs. Many approaches to enhancing productivity and quality reflect efforts to expand some of the job characteristics.[2]

Because of the effects of job design on performance, employee satisfaction, health, and many other factors, many organizations are changing or have already changed the design of some jobs. One movement that has affected the design and characteristics of jobs and work is **reengineering,** which is rethinking and redesigning work to improve cost, service, and speed. The reengineering process may include such techniques as creating work teams, training employees in multiple skills so they can do multiple jobs, pushing decision making as far down the organizational hierarchy as possible, and reorganizing operations and offices to simplify and speed work.

Teams and Jobs

Typically, a job is thought of as something done by one person. However, where it is appropriate, jobs may be designed for teams. In an attempt to make jobs more meaningful and to take advantage of the increased productivity and commitment that can follow, more organizations are using teams of employees instead of individuals for jobs. Some firms have gone as far as dropping the terms *workers* and *employees,* replacing them with *teammates, crew members, cast members,* and others that emphasize teamwork.

The **self-directed work team** is composed of individuals who are assigned a cluster of tasks, duties, and responsibilities to be accomplished. Unlike special-purpose teams, these teams become the regular entities in which team members work.

Advantages and Disadvantages of Team Jobs

Teams have been a popular part of job redesigns for much of the last two decades. Improved productivity, greater employee involvement, more widespread employee learning, and greater employee ownership of problems are among the potential benefits. Even *virtual teams* linked primarily through advanced technology can contribute despite geographical dispersion of essential employees. Virtual teams also can easily take advantage of previously unavailable expertise.[3]

But not everyone has been pleased with teams as a part of job design. In some cases employers find that teams work better with employees who are "group oriented." Many companies have used teamwork without much thought. Too often, teamwork can be a buzzword or "feel-good" device that may actually get in the way of good decisions. Further, compensating individual team members is often a problem since there are differences in individual's capabilities and performance.

JOB SATISFACTION AND ORGANIZATIONAL COMMITMENT

In its most basic sense, **job satisfaction** is a positive emotional state resulting from evaluating one's job experiences. Job *dissatisfaction* occurs when these expectations are not met. For example, if an employee expects clean and safe working conditions on the job, then the employee is likely to be dissatisfied if the workplace is dirty and dangerous.

Job satisfaction has many dimensions. Commonly noted facets include satisfaction with the work, wages, recognition, rapport with supervisors and co-workers, and chance for advancement. Each dimension contributes to an individual's overall feeling of satisfaction with the job itself, but the "job" is defined differently by different people. There is no simple formula for predicting a worker's satisfaction. Furthermore, the relationship between productivity and job satisfaction is not entirely clear. The critical factor is what employees expect from their jobs and what they are receiving as rewards from their jobs. Although job satisfaction itself is interesting and important, perhaps the "bottom line" is the impact that job satisfaction has on organizational commitment, which affects the goals of productivity, quality, and service.

If employees are committed to an organization, they are more likely to be more productive. **Organizational commitment** is the degree to which employees believe in and accept organizational goals and want to remain with the organization. A logical extension of organizational commitment focuses specifically on decisions to remain with or leave an organization and are reflected in employee absenteeism and turnover statistics. Individuals who are not as satisfied with their jobs or who are not as committed to the organization are more likely to withdraw from the organization, either occasionally through absenteeism or permanently through turnover.

Absenteeism

Employees can be absent from work for several reasons. Clearly, some absenteeism is unavoidable. This is usually referred to as *involuntary absenteeism*. However, much absenteeism is avoidable; it is called *voluntary absenteeism*. Often, a relatively small number of individuals in the workplace are responsible for a disproportionate share of the total absenteeism in an organization. Controlling voluntary absenteeism is easier if managers understand its causes more clearly. However, there are a variety of thoughts on reducing voluntary absenteeism. Organizational policies on absenteeism should be stated clearly in an employee handbook and stressed by supervisors and managers.

The policies and rules an organization uses to govern absenteeism may provide a clue to the effectiveness of its control. Absenteeism control options fall into three categories: (1) discipline, (2) positive reinforcement, and (3) a combination of both.

▶ Disciplinary approach: People who are absent the first time receive an oral warning: subsequent absences bring written warnings, suspension, and finally dismissal.
▶ Positive reinforcement approach: Employees earn cash, recognition, time off, or other rewards for meeting attendance standards.
▶ Combination approach: The employer rewards desired behaviors and punishes undesired behaviors. One of the most effective absenteeism control methods is to provide paid sick leave banks for employees to use.

Some firms have extended their policies to provide a *paid time off (PTO)* program in which vacation time, holidays, and sick leave for each employee are combined into a PTO account. Employees use days from their accounts at their discretion for illness, personal time, or vacation. If employees run out of days in their accounts, then they are not paid for any additional days missed.

Turnover

Like absenteeism, turnover is related to job dissatisfaction.[4] **Turnover** occurs when employees leave an organization and have to be replaced. Excessive turnover can be a very costly problem, with a major impact on productivity.

Turnover also is often classified as voluntary or involuntary. *Involuntary turnover* occurs when an employee is fired. *Voluntary turnover* occurs when an employee leaves by choice, which can be caused by many factors, including lack of challenge, better opportunity elsewhere, pay, supervision, geographic relocation, and pressure. Certainly, not all turnover is negative. Some workforce losses are quite desirable, especially if the workers leaving are lower-performing, less reliable individuals.

Turnover can be controlled in several ways:

▶ Good recruiting: use realistic job previews and avoid hiring employees who have a high probability of leaving
▶ Good initial employee orientation

▶ Competitive compensation
▶ Promotion from within
▶ Good supervision
▶ Adequate training
▶ Consistent HR policies

Even though some turnover is inevitable, organizations must take steps to control excessive turnover, particularly that caused by organizational factors such as poor supervision, inadequate training, and inconsistent policies. HR activities should be examined as part of the turnover control efforts.

ASSESSING HR EFFECTIVENESS

Productivity, quality, service, absenteeism, and turnover are all measurable—and they are related to the way activities are performed in an organization. HR—like marketing, legal, or finance—must be evaluated based on the value it adds to the organization. Defining and measuring HR effectiveness is not as straightforward as it might be in some more easily quantifiable areas, but it can be done. To demonstrate to the rest of the organization that the HR unit is a partner with a positive influence on the bottom line of the business, HR professionals must be prepared to measure the results of HR activities. Then the HR unit must communicate that information to the rest of the organization. Performance can come from several sources. Some of those sources are already available in most organizations, but some data may have to be collected. Records and data also can provide a crucial source of information to audit or assess the effectiveness of any unit. They provide the basis for research into possible causes of HR problems. Some examples of data from records can include the following:

▶ HR expense per employee
▶ Compensation as a percent of expenses

▶ HR department expense as a percent of total expenses
▶ Turnover rate
▶ Absence rate

HR Audits

One general means for assessing HR effectiveness is through an HR audit, similar to a financial audit. An HR audit is a formal research effort that evaluates the current status of HR management in an organization. Through the development and use of statistical reports and research data, HR audits attempt to evaluate how well HR activities have been performed, so that management can identify what needs to be improved.[5]

Employee Attitude Surveys

Employee opinions can be used to diagnose specific problem areas, identify employee needs or preferences, and reveal areas in which HR activities are well received or are viewed negatively. The **attitude survey** focuses on employees' feelings and beliefs about their jobs and the organization. By serving as a sounding board to allow employees to air their views about their jobs, their supervisors, their co-workers, and organizational policies and practices, these surveys can be starting points for improving job satisfaction. Some employers conduct attitude surveys on a regularly scheduled basis (such as every year), while others do so intermittently. As the use of e-mail has spread, more organizations have begun conducting attitude surveys electronically.

Exit Interviews

One widely used type of interview is the **exit interview**, in which those who are leaving the organization are asked to identify the reasons for their departure. This information can be used to correct problems so that others will not leave. HR specialists rather than supervisors usually conduct exit interviews, and a skilled HR interviewer can gain useful information. A wide range of issues can be examined in exit interviews, including reasons for leaving, supervision, pay, training, and the best-liked and least-liked aspects of the job.

HR Performance and Benchmarking

When information on HR performance has been gathered, it must be compared to a standard. A *standard* is a model or measure against which something is compared to determine its performance. For example, it is meaningless to know that the organizational turnover rate is 75% if it is not known what the turnover rates at comparable organizations might be. One approach to assessing HR effectiveness is **benchmarking**, which compares specific measures of performance against data on those measures in other "best practices" organizations. The most commonly benchmarked performance measures in HR management are the following:[6]

- ▶ Total compensation as a percentage of net income before taxes
- ▶ Percentage of management positions filled internally
- ▶ Dollar sales per employee
- ▶ Benefits as a percentage of payroll cost

A useful way to analyze HR involves calculating ratios. The ratios can be calculated and compared from year to year, providing information about changes

FIGURE 2-2 HR Ratios and Measures for Assessment

HR FUNCTION	USEFUL RATIOS	
• **Selection**	$\dfrac{\text{Long-term vacancies}}{\text{Total jobs}}$	$\dfrac{\text{Vacancies filled internally}}{\text{Total vacancies}}$
	$\dfrac{\text{Time to fill vacancy}}{\text{Total vacancies}}$	$\dfrac{\text{Offers accepted}}{\text{Offers extended}}$
• **Training**	$\dfrac{\text{Number of days training}}{\text{Number of employees}}$	$\dfrac{\text{Total training budget}}{\text{Total vacancies}}$
• **Compensation**	$\dfrac{\text{Total compensation costs}}{\text{Total revenue}}$	$\dfrac{\text{Basic salary cost}}{\text{Total compensation cost}}$
• **Employee relations**	$\dfrac{\text{Resignations}}{\text{Total employees per year}}$	$\dfrac{\text{Length of service}}{\text{Total employees}}$
	$\dfrac{\text{Absences}}{\text{Days worked per month}}$	$\dfrac{\text{Total managers}}{\text{Total employees}}$
• **Overall HR**	$\dfrac{\text{Part-time employees}}{\text{Total employees}}$	$\dfrac{\text{HR professionals}}{\text{Total employees}}$

in HR operations. For example, one suggested series of ratios and measures to consider is shown in Figure 2-2.

GLOBAL HUMAN RESOURCE MANAGEMENT

The internationalization of business has proceeded at a rapid pace as the world has become a global economy. Globalization has had a major impact on HR management. Managing human resources in different cultures, economies, and legal systems presents some challenges. However, when done well, effective global HR management pays dividends.

The most common obstacles to effective HR management are cross-cultural adaptation, different organizational/workforce values, differences in management style, and management turnover. Doing business globally requires that adaptations be made to reflect these factors. It is crucial that such concerns be seen as interrelated by managers and professionals as they do business and

FIGURE 2-3   Considerations Affecting Global HR Management

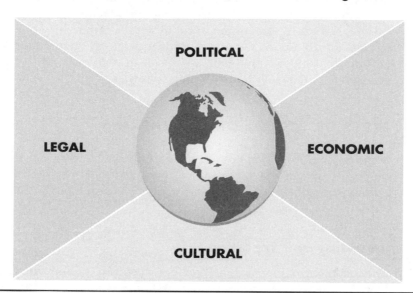

establish operations globally. Figure 2-3 depicts the general considerations for HR managers with global responsibilities. Each of these factors will be examined briefly.

Legal and Political Factors

The nature and stability of political systems vary from country to country. U.S. firms are accustomed to a relatively stable political system, and the same is true in many of the developed countries in Europe. However, in many other nations, the legal and political systems are turbulent. HR regulations and laws vary among countries in character and detail. In many countries, laws on labor unions and employment make it difficult to reduce the number of workers because required payments to former employees can be very high.

Economic Factors

Economic factors affect the other three factors in Figure 2-3. Different countries have different economic systems. Some even still operate with a modified version of communism. Because economic conditions vary greatly, the cost of living is a major economic consideration for global corporations.

Cultural Factors

Culture represents another important concern affecting international HR management. **Culture** is composed of the societal forces affecting the values, beliefs, and actions of a distinct group of people. Cultural differences certainly exist between nations, but significant cultural differences exist within countries also. One only has to look at the conflicts caused by religion or ethnicity in central Europe and other parts of the world to see the importance of culture in international organizations. Getting individuals from different ethnic or tribal backgrounds to work together may be difficult in some parts of the world. Culture can lead to ethical differences among countries.

TYPES OF GLOBAL ORGANIZATIONS

Some organizations that operate within only one country are recognizing that they must change and develop a more international perspective. Such organizations may pass through three stages as they broaden out into the world. A discussion of each stage follows.

Importing and Exporting

The first phase of international interaction consists of **importing and exporting**. Here, an organization begins selling and buying goods and services with organizations in other countries. Most of the international contacts are made by the sales and marketing staff and a limited number of other executives who negotiate contracts. Generally, HR activities are not affected except for travel policies for those going abroad.

Multinational Enterprises

As firms develop and expand, they identify opportunities to begin operating in other countries. A **multinational enterprise (MNE)** is one in which organizational units are located in foreign countries. Typically these units provide goods and services for the geographic areas surrounding the countries where operations exist. Key management positions in the foreign operations are filled with employees from the home country of the corporation. As the MNE expands, it hires workers from the countries in which it has operations. HR practices for employees sent from corporate headquarters must be developed so that these employees and their dependents may continue their economic lifestyles while stationed outside the home country.

Global Organizations

The MNE can be thought of as an *international* firm, in that it operates in various countries but each foreign business unit is operated separately. In contrast, a **global organization** has corporate units in a number of countries that are integrated to operate as one organization worldwide. An MNE may evolve into a global organization as operations in various countries become more integrated. HR management in truly global organizations moves people, especially key managers and professionals, throughout the world. Individuals who speak several languages fluently are highly valued, and they will move among divisions and countries as they assume more responsibilities and experience career growth. As much as possible, international HR management must be viewed strategically in these organizations. Global HR policies and activities are developed, but decentralization of decision making to subsidiary units and operations in other countries is necessary in order for country-specific adjustments to be made.

INTERNATIONAL STAFFING AND TRAINING

Deciding on the mix of local employees, employees from the home country, and even people from third countries that will best meet organizational goals is a challenge. In staffing an overseas operation, cost is a major consideration.

Types of International Employees

International employees can be placed in three different classifications.

- ▶ An **expatriate** is an employee working in a unit or plant who is not a citizen of the country in which the unit or plant is located, but is a citizen of the country in which the organization is headquartered.
- ▶ A **host-country national** is an employee working in a unit or plant who is a citizen of the country in which the unit or plant is located, when the unit or plant is operated by an organization headquartered in another country.
- ▶ A **third-country national** is a citizen of one country, working in a second country, and employed by an organization headquartered in a third country.

Each of these individuals presents some HR management challenges. Because in a given situation each is a citizen of a different country, different tax laws and other factors apply. HR professionals have to be knowledgeable about the laws and customs of each country. They must establish appropriate payroll and record-keeping procedures, among other activities, to ensure compliance with varying regulations and requirements.

Selection for International Assignments

The selection process for an international assignment should provide a realistic picture of the life, work, and culture where the employee may be sent. HR managers should prepare a comprehensive description of the job to be done. This description especially should note responsibilities that would be unusual in the home nation, including negotiating with public officials; interpreting local work codes; and responding to ethical, moral, and personal issues such as religious prohibitions and personal freedoms. Most staffing "failures" among those placed in foreign assignments occur because of cultural adjustment problems, not because of difficulties with the jobs or inadequate technical skills.

FIGURE 2-4 International Training and Development

Organizational support for employees is particularly important for successful cultural adjustment. One of the most basic skills needed by expatriate employees is the ability to communicate orally and in writing in the host-country language. Inability to communicate adequately in the language may significantly inhibit the success of an expatriate.

The preferences and attitudes of spouses and other family members also are major staffing considerations. Two of the most common reasons for turning down international assignments are family considerations and spouses' careers.

International Training and Development

In any organization—global in scope or not—training and development are key factors for HR success. For the global firm these activities are just as important, but for incoming expatriates, host-country nationals, and third-country nationals, training and development is crucial. Figure 2-4 shows three different kinds of training and development activities for global employees. Not all apply to every type of international employee, but all are important.

Predeparture Orientation and Training. The orientation and training that expatriates and their families receive before departure have a major impact on the success of the overseas assignment. Three areas affect the cross-cultural adjustment process: (1) work adjustment, (2) interaction adjustment, and (3) general adjustment. Permeating all of those areas is the need for training in foreign language and culture familiarization. Many firms have formal training programs for expatriates and their families, and this training has been found to have a positive effect on cross-cultural adjustment.

Continuing Employee Training and Development. Career planning and continued involvement of expatriates in corporate employee development activities are essential. One of the greatest deterrents to accepting foreign assignments is employees' concerns that they will be "out of sight, out of mind." If they do not have direct and regular contact with others at the corporate headquarters, many expatriates experience anxiety about their continued career progression. Therefore, the international experiences of expatriates must be seen as beneficial to the employer and to the expatriate's career.

Repatriation Training and Development. The process of bringing expatriates home is called **repatriation**. Some major difficulties can arise when it is time to bring expatriates home. Often, expatriates have a greater degree of flexibility, autonomy, and independent decision making than do their counterparts in the United States. Expatriates often must be reacclimatized to U.S. lifestyles, transportation services, and other cultural practices, especially if they have been living in less developed countries.

INTERNATIONAL COMPENSATION AND OTHER ACTIVITIES

Organizations with employees in many different countries face some special compensation pressures. Variations in laws, living costs, tax policies, and other factors all must be considered in establishing the compensation for expatriate managers and professionals. Even fluctuations in the value of the U.S. dollar must be tracked and adjustments made as the dollar rises or falls in relation to currency rates in other countries. Add to all of these concerns the need to compensate employees for the costs of housing, schooling of children, and yearly transportation home for themselves and their family members. When all these different issues are considered, it is evident that international compensation is extremely complex.

Many multinational firms have compensation programs that make use of the **balance-sheet approach**. This approach provides international employees with a compensation package that equalizes cost differences between the international assignment and the same assignment in the home country of the individual or the corporation.

Increasingly, global organizations have recognized that attracting, retaining, and motivating managers with global capabilities requires taking a broader perspective than just sending expatriates overseas. As mentioned earlier, in many large multinational enterprises, key executives have worked in several countries and may be of many different nationalities. These executives are moved from one part of the world to another and to corporate headquarters wherever the firms are based. It appears that there is a high demand for these global managers, and they almost form their own "global market" for compensation purposes.

Many international compensation plans attempt to protect expatriates from negative tax consequences by using a **tax equalization plan**. Under this plan, the company adjusts an employee's base income downward by the amount of estimated U.S. tax to be paid for the year. Thus, the employee pays only the foreign-country tax. The intent of the tax equalization plan is to ensure that expatriates will not pay any more or less in taxes than if they had stayed in the United States.

International Security and Terrorism

As more U.S. firms operate internationally, the threat of terrorist actions against those firms and the employees working for them increases. U.S. citizens are especially vulnerable to extortions, kidnapping, bombing, physical harassment, and other terrorist activities. In a three-month period in a recent year, several hundred terrorist acts were aimed at businesses and businesspeople. Many of these acts targeted company facilities and offices. Nevertheless, individual employees and their families living abroad must constantly be aware of security issues.

Global Labor-Management Relations

The strength and nature of unions differ from country to country. In some countries, unions either do not exist at all or are relatively weak. In other countries, unions are extremely strong and are closely tied to political parties. Some countries require that firms have union or worker representatives on their boards of directors. This practice is very common in European countries, where it is called **co-determination**.

Behind the hype and the horror stories, there is one valid generalization about foreign assignments: They can pay professional and personal dividends, but they carry some real risks. The organizations that help their expatriates deal with the risks—and choose the right people for those very challenging assignments—ultimately benefit.

NOTES

1. Keith Whitefield and Michael Poole, "Organizing Employment for High Performance," *Organization Studies,* Winter 1997, 745.
2. Joan Rentsch and Robert Steel, "Testing the Durability of Job Characteristics as Predictors of Absenteeism over a Six-Year Period," *Personnel Psychology* 51, 1998, 165.
3. Anthony Townsend, Samuel DeMarie, and Anthony Hendrickson, "Virtual Teams: Technology and the Workplace of the Future," *Academy of Management Executive,* August 1998, 17.
4. Rodger W. Griffeth et al., "Comparative Tests of Multivariate Models of Recruiting Source Effects," *Journal of Management* 23, 1997.
5. Mark Spoginardi, "Conducting a Human Resources Audit—A Primer," *Employee Relations Law Journal* 23, 1997, 105.
6. "Compare Your Company to These Performance-Management Benchmarks," *IOMA's Pay for Performance Report,* January 1998, 1.

SUGGESTED READINGS

Anne Bruce and James S. Pepitone, *Motivating Employees,* McGraw-Hill, 1999.

Farid Elashmawi and Philip R. Harris, *Multicultural Management 2000,* Gulf Publishing, 2000.

Joyce L. Gioia and Roger E. Herman, *How to Become an Employer of Choice,* Oak Hill Press, 2000.

Calvin Reynolds, *The 2000 Guide to Global Compensation and Benefits,* Harcourt, Inc., 1999.

Scott S. Rodrick, *Equity-Based Compensation for Multinational Corporations,* The National Center for Employee Ownership, 1999.

SUGGESTED INTERNET RESOURCES

International Telework Association & Council. Describes telecommuting programs, issues and ways to make it successful.

http://www.telecommute.org

Expat Forum. Contains suggestions and information on HR issues associated with managing expatriate employees.

http://www.expatforum.com

CHAPTER 3

Equal Employment Opportunity

Organizations today have a more diverse workforce. Managing diversity and ensuring equal employment opportunity for all employees is vital, especially given all of the laws and regulations in existence.

People are different on many dimensions, as Figure 3-1 shows. Age, gender, and race are only a few. The concept of *diversity* recognizes the differences among people. The existence of diversity is apparent in most organizations. As suggested in a number of studies, diversity has both positive and negative consequences. On the positive side, it provides organizations opportunities to tap a broader, more diverse set of people, ideas, and experiences. On the negative side, diversity may initially lead to increased tensions and conflicts in the workplace. Consequently, organizations must be *proactive* both in addressing diversity concerns of existing employees and in supporting individuals with different backgrounds and heritages.

DIVERSITY

Diversity is seen in demographic differences in the workforce. The shifting makeup of the U.S. population accounts for today's increased workforce diversity as many organizations hire from a more diverse pool of potential workers. Organizations have been seeing the effects of changing demographic trends for several years. A more detailed look at some of the key changes follows. According to the U.S. Department of Labor:[1]

▶ Total workforce growth will be slower between 2000 and 2006 than in previous decades.
▶ Only one-third of the entrants to the workforce between 2000 and 2005 will be white males.

FIGURE 3-1 **Dimensions of Diversity**

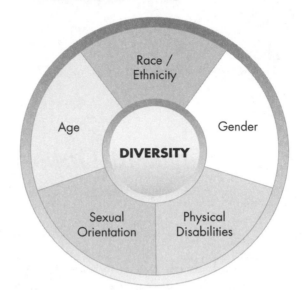

▶ Women will constitute a greater proportion of the labor force than in the past, and 63% of all U.S. women will be in the workforce by 2005.
▶ Minority racial and ethnic groups will account for a growing percentage of the overall labor force. Immigrants will expand this growth.
▶ The average age of the U.S. population will increase, and more workers who retire from full-time jobs will work part time.
▶ As a result of these and other shifts, employers in a variety of industries will face shortages of qualified workers.

Women in the Workforce

The influx of women into the workforce has major social and economic consequences. Implications for HR management of more women working include the following:

▶ Greater flexibility in work patterns and schedules to accommodate women with family responsibilities, part-time work interests, or other pressures.
▶ More variety in benefits programs and HR policies, including child-care assistance and parental leave programs.
▶ Greater employer awareness of gender-related legal issues such as sexual harassment and sex discrimination.

Racial and Ethnic Diversity in the Workforce

The fastest-growing segments of the U.S. population are minority racial and ethnic groups, especially Hispanic Americans, African Americans, and Asian Americans. Possible implications of the increase in racial and ethnic cultural diversity are as follows:

- ▶ The potential for work-related conflicts among various racial and ethnic groups could increase.
- ▶ Extensive employer-sponsored cultural awareness and diversity training may be required to defuse conflicts and promote multicultural understanding.
- ▶ Job training will have to accommodate the different language abilities of a multicultural workforce.
- ▶ Greater cultural diversity in dress, customs, and lifestyles will be seen in workplaces.

Aging of the Workforce

Most of the developed countries—including Australia, Japan, most European countries, and the United States—are experiencing an aging of their populations. Implications of the aging of the U.S. workforce include the following:

- ▶ Retirement will change in character as organizations and older workers choose phased retirements, early retirement buyouts, and part-time work.
- ▶ Service industries will actively recruit senior workers for many jobs.
- ▶ Retirement benefits will increase in importance, particularly pension and health-care coverage for retirees.

Individuals with Disabilities in the Workforce

With the passage of the Americans with Disabilities Act (ADA) in 1990, employers were reminded of their responsibilities for employing individuals with disabilities. At least forty-three million Americans with disabilities are covered by the ADA. Implications of greater employment of individuals with disabilities include the following:

- ▶ Employers must define more precisely what are the essential tasks in jobs and what knowledge, skills, and abilities are needed to perform each job.
- ▶ Accommodating individuals with disabilities will become more common as employers provide more flexible work schedules, altering facilities, and purchasing special equipment.
- ▶ Employment-related health and medical examination requirements will be revised to avoid discriminating against individuals with disabilities.

Individuals with Differing Sexual Orientations in the Workforce

A growing number of employers are facing legislative efforts to protect individuals with differing sexual orientations from employment discrimination, though at present only a few cities and states have passed such laws. Implications of these issues include the following:

FIGURE 3-2 **Major Components of Successful Diversity Management**

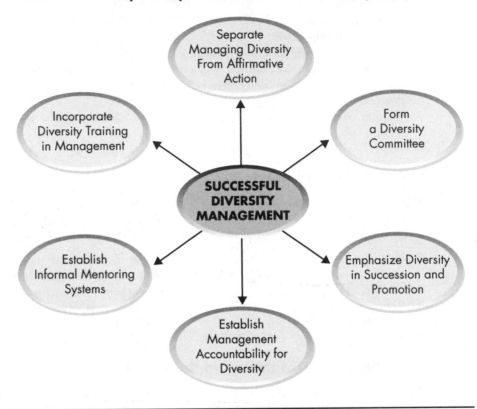

▶ The potential for workplace conflicts is heightened as people with different lifestyles and sexual orientations work together. Training to reduce such workplace conflicts will be necessary.

▶ Generally, managers must recognize that they should not attempt to "control" off-the-job behavior of employees unless it has a direct, negative effect on the organization.

MANAGING DIVERSITY

Failure to manage the potential difficulties associated with diversity can lead to problems. There are many different sources of advice and opinions about how to approach the challenges of diversity in an organization. Figure 3-2 summarizes the most commonly cited components of diversity management efforts. Roughly three-fourths of the Fortune 500 companies have diversity programs. Smaller companies have diversity programs as well, but only about one-third of the smaller companies have such programs.[2]

Diversity training seeks to eliminate infringements on legal rights, and to minimize discrimination, harassment, and lawsuits. Approaches to diversity training vary, but often include at least three components:

▶ *Legal awareness:* Typically addresses federal and state laws and regulations on equal employment, and examines consequences of violations of those laws and regulations.
▶ *Cultural awareness:* Attempts to deal with stereotypes, typically through discussion and exercises.
▶ *Sensitivity training:* Aims at "sensitizing" people to the differences among them and how their words and behaviors are seen by others. Some training includes exercises containing examples of harassing and other behaviors. These exercises are designed to show white males how discrimination feels.

Although diversity training is designed to correct problems, in many cases it appears to have made them worse. In both public- and private-sector organizations, mixed reviews about the effectiveness of diversity training suggest that either the programs or their implementations are suspect.[3]

EQUAL EMPLOYMENT OPPORTUNITY AND AFFIRMATIVE ACTION

Equal employment opportunity (EEO) is a broad concept holding that individuals should have equal treatment in all employment-related actions. Individuals who are covered under equal employment laws are protected from illegal discrimination, which occurs when individuals having a common characteristic are discriminated against based on that characteristic. Various laws have been passed to protect individuals who share certain characteristics, such as race, age, or gender. Those having the designated characteristics are referred to as members of a **protected class**. The following bases for protection have been identified by various federal laws:

▶ Race, ethnic origin, color (African Americans, Hispanic Americans, Native Americans, Asian Americans)
▶ Gender (women, including those who are pregnant)
▶ Age (individuals over age 40)
▶ Individuals with disabilities (physical or mental)
▶ Military experience (Vietnam-era veterans)
▶ Religion (special beliefs and practices)

Affirmative Action

To remedy areas in which it appears that individuals in protected classes have not had equal employment opportunities, some employers have developed affirmative action policies. **Affirmative action** occurs when employers identify problem areas, set goals, and take positive steps to guarantee equal employment opportunities for people in a protected class. Affirmative action focuses on hiring, training, and promoting protected-class members where they are *under-represented* in an organization in relation to their availability in the labor markets from which recruiting occurs. Sometimes employers have instituted affirmative action voluntarily, but many times employers have been required to do so because they are government contractors with more than fifty employees and more than $50,000 in government contracts annually.

Reverse Discrimination

When equal employment opportunity regulations are discussed, probably the most volatile issue concerns the view that affirmative action leads to *quotas, preferential selection,* and *reverse discrimination.* At the heart of the conflict is the employer's role in selecting, training, and promoting protected-class members when they are underrepresented in various jobs in an organization. Those who are not members of any protected class have claimed that there is discrimination in reverse. This **reverse discrimination** may exist when a person is denied an opportunity because of preferences given to a member of a protected class who may be less qualified. Specifically, some critics charge that white males are at a disadvantage today, even though they traditionally have held many of the better jobs. Affirmative action as a concept is under attack by courts and employers, as well as by males and nonminorities. Whether that trend continues will depend on future changes in the makeup of the U.S. Supreme Court and the results of presidential and congressional elections. The authors of this text believe that whether one supports or opposes affirmative action, it is important to understand both why its supporters believe that it is needed and why its opponents believe it should be discontinued.

Civil Rights Acts of 1964 and 1991

Numerous federal, state, and local laws address equal employment opportunity concerns (see Appendix D). At this point, it is important to discuss two major broad-based civil rights acts that encompass many areas.

Civil Rights Act of 1964, Title VII. Although the first civil rights act was passed in 1866, it was not until the passage of the Civil Rights Act of 1964 that the keystone of antidiscrimination legislation was put into place. The Civil Rights Act of 1964 was passed in part to bring about equality in all employment-related decisions. As is often the case, the law contains ambiguous provisions giving considerable leeway to agencies that enforce the law. The Equal Employment Opportunity Commission (EEOC) was established to enforce the provisions of Title VII, the portion of the act that deals with employment.

Civil Rights Act of 1991. Several U.S. Supreme Court decisions made it more difficult for protected-class individuals to use statistics to show that illegal discrimination had occurred. The 1991 act reversed those rulings. The Civil Rights

Act of 1991 requires employers to demonstrate that an employment practice is *job-related for the position* and is consistent with *business necessity*. The act did clarify that the plaintiffs bringing the discrimination charges must identify the particular employer practice being challenged. *Can prove a Test given to potential employee is discriminating. must be job related.*

Enforcement Agencies

Government agencies at several levels have powers to investigate illegal discriminatory practices. At the state and local levels, various commissions have enforcement authority. At the federal level, the two most prominent agencies are the Equal Employment Opportunity Commission (EEOC) and the Office of Federal Contract Compliance Programs (OFCCP). *→ for employers that deal w/ Federal contracts*

The EEOC, created by the Civil Rights Act of 1964, is responsible for enforcing the employment-related provisions of the act. The agency initiates investigations, responds to complaints, and develops guidelines to enforce various laws.

While the EEOC is an independent agency, the OFCCP is part of the Department of Labor, established by Executive Order to ensure that federal contractors and subcontractors have nondiscriminatory practices. A major thrust of OFCCP efforts is to require that federal contractors and subcontractors take affirmative action to overcome the effects of prior discriminatory practices.

Interpretations of EEO Laws and Regulations

Laws establishing the legal basis for equal employment opportunity generally have been written broadly. Consequently, only through application to specific organizational situations can one see how the laws affect employers. Discrimination can be illegal in employment-related situations in which either (1) different standards are used to judge different individuals, or (2) the same standard is used, but it is not related to the individuals' jobs. When deciding if and when illegal discrimination has occurred, courts and regulatory agencies have had to consider the issue of disparate treatment and disparate impact.

Disparate treatment occurs when protected-class members are treated differently from others. For example, if female applicants must take a special skills test not given to male applicants, then disparate treatment may be occurring. If disparate treatment has occurred, the courts generally have said that intentional discrimination exists. *intentional or not →*

Disparate impact occurs when there is substantial underrepresentation of protected-class members as a result of employment decisions that work to their disadvantage. The landmark case that established the importance of disparate impact as a legal foundation of EEO law is *Griggs v. Duke Power* (1971).[4]

EEO Compliance

Employers must comply with EEO regulations and guidelines. To do so, management should have an EEO policy statement and maintain all required EEO-related records. It is crucial that all employers have a written EEO policy statement. This policy should be widely disseminated throughout the organization. All employers with fifteen or more employees are required to keep certain records that can be requested by the EEOC. The basic report that must be filed with the EEOC is the annual report form EEO-1.

Pre-Employment versus After-Hire Inquiries. Appendix E lists pre-employment inquiries and identifies whether they may or may not be discriminatory. Once an employer tells an applicant he or she is hired (the "point of hire"), inquiries that were prohibited earlier may be made. After hiring, medical examination forms, group insurance cards, and other enrollment cards containing inquiries related directly or indirectly to sex, age, or other bases may be requested. Photographs or evidence of race, religion, or national origin also may be requested after hire for legal and necessary purposes, but not before. Such data should be maintained in a separate personnel records system in order to avoid their use in making appraisal, discipline, termination, or promotion decisions.

Who Must Have an Affirmative Action Plan? Generally, an employer with at least _fifty employees_ and over _$50,000 in federal government contracts_ must have a formal, written affirmative action plan (AAP). The contents of an AAP and the policies flowing from it must be available for review by managers and supervisors within the organization. Plans vary in length; some are long and require extensive staff time to prepare.

Small business don't have to comply

UNIFORM GUIDELINES ON EMPLOYEE SELECTION PROCEDURES

The Uniform Guidelines on Employee Selection Procedures were developed by the EEOC, the U.S. Department of Labor's OFCCP, the U.S. Department of Justice, and the Office of Personnel Management. The guidelines provide a framework used to determine whether employers are adhering to federal laws on discrimination. The guidelines apply to most employment-related decisions, not just to the initial hiring process.[5] The major means of compliance identified by the guidelines are (1) no disparate impact and (2) job-related validation.

"No-Disparate-Impact" Approach — 4/5 Rule

How many applied & how many were hired (black vs. white)

Under the guidelines, disparate impact is determined with the **4/5ths rule**. If the selection rate for any protected group is less than 80% (4/5ths) of the selection rate for the majority group or less than 80% of the group's representation in the relevant labor market, discrimination exists. Thus, the guidelines have attempted to define discrimination in statistical terms.

Job-Related Validation Approach

Under the job-related validation approach, virtually every factor used to make employment-related decisions—recruiting, selection, promotion, termination, discipline, and performance appraisal—must be shown to be specifically job-related. **Validity** is simply the extent to which a test actually measures what it says it measures. An employment test that is valid must measure the person's ability to perform the job for which he or she is being hired.

The ideal condition for employment-related tests is to be both valid and reliable. **Reliability** refers to the consistency with which a test measures an item. For a test to be reliable, an individual's score should be about the same every time the individual takes the test (allowing for the effects of practice). Unless a test measures a trait consistently (or reliably), it is of little value in predicting job performance.

The 1978 Uniform Selection Guidelines recognize three types of validation:

- ▶ Content validity — *logical non statistical method ex. typing test*
- ▶ Criterion-related validity (concurrent and predictive) *ex. test/workers = test work grade = performance*
- ▶ Construct validity

Content validity is a logical, nonstatistical method used to identify the knowledge, skills, and abilities (KSAs) and other characteristics necessary to perform a job. A test has content validity if it reflects an actual sample of the work done on the job in question. There are two approaches to criterion-related validity. When an employer measures **concurrent validity**, a test is given to current employees and the scores are correlated with their job performance. A high correlation suggests that the test can differentiate between the better-performing employees and those with poor performance records. To measure **predictive validity**, test results of applicants are compared with their subsequent job performance. However, predictive validity requires (1) a fairly large number of people (usually at least thirty) and (2) a time gap between the test and the performance (usually one year). As a result, predictive validity is not practical in many situations. Because of these and other problems, other types of validity often are used.

Construct validity shows a relationship between an abstract characteristic inferred from research and job performance. These are called *constructs*. Examples of psychological constructs are **motivation** and **learning**.

GENDER DISCRIMINATION AND SEXUAL HARASSMENT

Title VII of the Civil Rights Act of 1964 prohibits discrimination in employment on the basis of gender. Other laws and regulations are aimed at eliminating such discrimination in specific areas. As more men and women work together in teams and on projects, more employers are becoming concerned about personal relationships between employees. This section begins with a discussion of sexual harassment and then discusses other forms of gender-based discrimination.

Sexual Harassment

The EEOC has issued guidelines designed to curtail sexual harassment. The two types of sexual harassment are defined as follows:

"this that" for

▶ *Quid pro quo* harassment occurs when an employer or supervisor links specific employment outcomes to the individuals' granting sexual favors.

▶ *Hostile environment* harassment occurs when the harassment has the effect of unreasonably interfering with work performance or psychological well-being or when intimidating or offensive working conditions are created.

Linking any condition of employment—including pay raises, promotions, assignments of work and work hours, performance appraisals, meetings, disciplinary actions, and many others—to the granting of sexual favors can be the basis for a charge of *quid pro quo* ("something for something") harassment. Certainly, harassment by supervisors and managers who expect sexual favors as a condition for a raise or promotion is inappropriate behavior in a work environment. This view has been supported in a wide variety of cases.

The second type of sexual harassment involves the creation of a hostile work environment. In *Harris v. Forklift Systems, Inc.,* the U.S. Supreme Court ruled that in determining if a hostile environment exists, the following factors should be considered.[6]

▶ Whether the conduct was physically threatening or humiliating, rather than just offensive

▶ Whether the conduct interfered unreasonably with an employee's work performance

▶ Whether the conduct affected the employee's psychological well-being

Reasonable Care. Employers should ensure "reasonable care" in their HR policies and practices by:

▶ Establishing a sexual harassment policy

▶ Communicating the policy regularly

▶ Training all employees, especially supervisors and managers, on avoiding sexual harassment

▶ Investigating and taking action when complaints are voiced

Prompt action by the employer to investigate sexual harassment complaints and then to punish the identified harassers aid an employer's defense. If harassment situations are taken seriously by employers, the ultimate outcomes are more likely to be favorable for them.

Pregnancy Discrimination

The Pregnancy Discrimination Act (PDA) of 1978 was passed as an amendment to the Civil Rights Act of 1964. Its major provision was that any employer with fifteen or more employees had to treat maternity leave the same as other personal or medical leaves. Closely related to the PDA is the Family and Medical Leave Act (FMLA) of 1993, which requires that individuals be given up to twelve weeks of family leave without pay based on several different situations and also requires that those taking family leave be allowed to return to jobs. The FMLA applies to both men and women.

Equal Pay and Pay Equity

The Equal Pay Act, enacted in 1963, requires employers to pay similar wage rates for similar work without regard to gender. Tasks performed intermittently or infrequently do not make jobs different enough to justify significantly different wages. Differences in pay may be allowed because of (1) differences in seniority, (2) differences in performance, (3) differences in quality and/or quantity of production, and (4) factors other than sex, such as skill, effort, and working conditions.

According to the concept of **pay equity**, the pay for jobs requiring comparable levels of knowledge, skill, and ability should be similar even if actual duties differ significantly. This concept has also been called *comparable worth* when earlier cases were addressed. The Equal Pay Act applies to jobs that are substantially the same, whereas pay equity applies to jobs that are valued similarly in the organization, whether or not they are the same.

The "Glass Ceiling"

For years, women's groups have alleged that women encounter a glass ceiling in the workplace. The **glass ceiling** refers to discriminatory practices that have prevented women and other protected-class members from advancing to executive-level jobs. A related problem is that women have tended to advance to senior management in a limited number of functional areas, such as human resources and corporate communications. Because jobs in these "supporting" areas tend to pay less than jobs in sales, marketing, operations, or finance, the overall impact is to reduce women's career progression and income. Limits that keep women from progressing only in certain fields have been referred to as "glass walls" or "glass elevators." Some firms have established formal mentoring programs in order to break down glass walls.

AGE DISCRIMINATION

The Age Discrimination in Employment Act (ADEA) of 1967, amended in 1978 and 1986, makes it illegal for an employer to discriminate in compensation, terms, conditions, or privileges of employment because of an individual's age. The later amendments first raised the minimum mandatory retirement age of 70 and then eliminated it completely. The ADEA applies to all individuals over age 40 working for employers with twenty or more workers. However, the act does not apply if age is a job-related occupational qualification.

The Older Workers Benefit Protection Act (OWBPA) of 1990 was passed to amend the ADEA to ensure that equal treatment for older workers occurs in early retirement or severance situations. Many early retirement and downsizing efforts by employers target older workers by hoping to entice them to choose early retirement buyouts and enhanced severance packages. In exchange, employers often require the workers to sign waivers indicating that by accepting the retirement incentives, the workers waive their rights to sue the employers for age discrimination. The OWBPA provides regulations on the use of these waivers.

AMERICANS WITH DISABILITIES ACT (ADA)

The passage of the Americans with Disabilities Act (ADA) in 1990 represented an expansion in the scope of impact of laws and regulations on discrimination against individuals with disabilities. The ADA contains the following requirements dealing with employment.

▶ Discrimination is prohibited against individuals with disabilities who can perform the essential job functions, a standard that is somewhat vague.
▶ A covered employer must have reasonable accommodation for people with disabilities, so that they can function as employees, unless undue hardship would be placed on the employer.
▶ Pre-employment medical examinations are prohibited except after a conditional employment offer is made.

As defined by the ADA, a disabled person is someone who has a physical or mental impairment that substantially limits that person in some major life activities, who has a record of such an impairment, or who is regarded as having such an impairment. A growing area of concern under the ADA is individuals with mental disabilities. Generally employers have prevailed when charges of discrimination against a person with a mental disability have been brought against them. A mental illness is often more difficult to diagnose than a physical disability. In an attempt to add clarification, the EEOC has released explanatory guidelines, but the situations are still confusing.[7]

Essential Job Functions

The ADA requires that the **essential job functions** be identified in written job descriptions that indicate the amount of time spent performing various functions and their criticality. Most employers have interpreted this provision to mean that they should develop and maintain current and comprehensive job descriptions for all jobs.

Reasonable Accommodation

A reasonable accommodation is a modification or adjustment to a job or work environment that enables a qualified individual with a disability to have equal employment opportunity. Employers are required to provide reasonable accommodation for individuals with disabilities to ensure that legal discrimination does not occur.

Undue Hardship

Reasonable accommodation is restricted to actions that do not place an **undue hardship** on an employer. An action places undue hardship on an employer if it imposes significant difficulty or expense. The ADA offers only general guidelines on when an accommodation becomes unreasonable and places undue hardship on an employer.

OTHER BASES OF DISCRIMINATION

There are several other bases of discrimination that various laws have identified as illegal. This area continues to be an expanding concern to employers.

Immigration Reform and Control Act (IRCA)

To deal with problems arising from the continued flow of immigrants to the United States, the Immigration Reform and Control Act (IRCA) was passed in 1986 and has been revised in later years. The IRCA makes it illegal for an employer to discriminate in recruiting, hiring, or terminating based on an individual's national origin or citizenship. Recent revisions to the IRCA changed some of the restrictions on the entry of immigrants to work in U.S. organizations, particularly those organizations with high-technology and other "scarce-skills" areas. Employers are required to examine identification documents for new employees, who also must sign verification forms about their eligibility to work legally in the United States.

Religious Discrimination

Title VII of the Civil Rights Act identifies discrimination on the basis of religion as illegal. However, religious schools and institutions can use religion as a bona fide occupational qualification (BFOQ) for employment practices on a limited scale.

Sexual Orientation

Some states and cities have passed laws prohibiting discrimination based on sexual orientation or lifestyle. Even the issue of benefits coverage for "domestic partners," whether heterosexual or homosexual, has been the subject of state and city legislation.

Veterans' Employment Rights

The employment rights of military veterans and reservists have been addressed by the passage of the Vietnam-Era Veterans Readjustment Act. The act requires that affirmative action in hiring and advancing Vietnam-era veterans be undertaken by federal contractors and subcontractors with contracts of $10,000 or more.

Military Employment Rights

Under the Uniformed Services Employment and Reemployment Rights Act of 1994, employees are required to notify their employers of military service obligations. Employees serving in the military must be provided leaves of absence and have reemployment rights for up to five years. Other provisions protect the right to benefits of employees called to military duty.

NOTES

1. U.S. Department of Labor, Bureau of Labor Statistics, 2001.
2. "SHRM Releases New Survey on Diversity Programs," *Mosaics*, July/August 1998, 1.
3. Gillian Flynn, "The Harsh Reality of Diversity Programs," *Workforce*, December 1998, 26–35.
4. *Griggs v. Duke Power Co.*, 401 U.S. 424 (1971).
5. "Adoption by Four Agencies of Uniform Guidelines on Employee Selection Procedures (1978)," *Federal Register*, August 15, 1978, Part IV, 38295-38309.
6. *Harris v. Forklift Systems, Inc.*, 114 S.Ct. 367 (1993).
7. Timothy Bland, "ADA: The Law Meets Medicine," *HR Magazine*, January 1999, 99–104.

SUGGESTED READINGS

John F. Buckley, *Equal Employment Opportunity: 2000 Compliance Guide*, Aspen Publishing, 2000.

Richard T. Seymour and Barbara B. Brown, *Equal Employment Law Update*, Bureau of National Affairs, 2000.

SHRM, *Preventing Harassment*, SHRM, 1999.

R. Roosevelt Thomas, *Building a House for Diversity*, AMACOM, 1999.

SUGGESTED INTERNET RESOURCES

U.S. Equal Employment Opportunity Commission. Contains news, studies, and information on equal employment.
http://www.eeoc.gov

American Institute for Managing Diversity. Describes diversity issues and the importance of addressing workforce diversity.
http://www.aimd.org

CHAPTER 4

Job Analysis

Both workers and jobs in organizations change over time. An understanding of what is occurring in jobs in organizations is developed through job analysis and the development of job descriptions and job specifications.

Because organizations are changing and jobs vary in different organizations, managers and employees alike are finding that designing and analyzing jobs requires greater attention than in the past. Analyzing and understanding the work done in the organization must be based on facts and data, not just personal perceptions of managers, supervisors, and employees. It has become evident in many organizations that analyzing what employees do in their jobs is vital to maintaining organizational competitiveness.

NATURE OF JOB ANALYSIS

The most basic building block of HR management, **job analysis**, is a systematic way to gather and analyze information about the content and human requirement of jobs, and the context in which jobs are performed. Job analysis usually involves collecting information on the characteristics of a job that differentiate it from other jobs. Information that can be helpful in making the distinction includes the following:

- Work activities and behaviors
- Interactions with others
- Performance standards
- Financial and budgeting impact
- Machines and equipment used
- Working conditions
- Supervision given and received
- Knowledge, skills, and abilities needed

how critical is a mistake?

Although the terms *job* and *position* are often used interchangeably, there is a slight difference in emphasis. A **job** is a grouping of common tasks, duties, and responsibilities. A **position** is a job performed by one person. Thus, if there are two people operating word processing equipment, there are two positions (one for each person) but just one job (word processing operator).

Work Analysis

Work analysis studies the workflow, activities, context, and output of a job. This analysis can be conducted on a department, business process, or individual level. At one level, the industrial engineering approach of time and motion studies is useful in work analysis. At another level, what is done in one department can be looked at in relation to work activities performed elsewhere in the organization. Analyzing work activities and processes may require looking at what capabilities individuals need as well as what they do. That certainly would be true as office support jobs, such as the secretarial job, are examined. Increasingly, it is being recognized that jobs can be analyzed on the basis of both tasks and competencies.

Task-Based Job Analysis

Analyzing jobs based upon what is done on the job focuses on the tasks, duties, and responsibilities performed in a job. A **task** is a distinct, identifiable work activity composed of motions, whereas a **duty** is a larger work segment composed of several tasks that are performed by an individual. Because both tasks and duties describe activities, it is not always easy or necessary to distinguish between the two. For example, if one of the employment supervisor's duties is to interview applicants, one task associated with that duty would be asking questions. **Job responsibilities** are obligations to perform certain tasks and duties.

Competency Approach to Job Analysis

There is a growing interest in focusing on the competencies that individuals need in order to perform jobs, rather than on the tasks, duties, and responsibilities composing a job. This shift emphasizes that it is the capabilities that people have that truly influence organizational performance. Instead of thinking of individuals having jobs that are relatively stable and can be written up into typical job descriptions, it may be more relevant to focus on the competencies used. **Competencies** are basic characteristics that can be linked to enhanced performance by individuals or teams of individuals. The groupings of competencies may include knowledge, skills, and abilities.

The competency approach considers how the knowledge and skills are used. The competency approach also attempts to identify the hidden factors that are often critical to superior performance. For instance, many supervisors talk about employees' attitudes, but they have difficulty identifying what they mean by *attitude.* The competency approach uses some methodologies to help supervisors identify examples of what they mean by attitude and how those factors affect performance. Examples of the competencies used in organizations vary widely, but they often include the following:

- ▶ Team orientation
- ▶ Technical expertise
- ▶ Leadership
- ▶ Adaptability

The competency approach focuses on linking business strategies to individual performance efforts. It also encourages employees to develop competencies that may be used in diverse work situations, rather than being boxed into a job. Development of employees focuses on enhancing their competencies, rather than preparing them for moving to specific jobs. In this way they can develop capabilities useful throughout the organization as it changes and evolves.

Ultimately, job analysis may change in order to address the changing nature of broader and looser jobs in some areas, while continuing to be relevant in areas where jobs remain task-based. Because the task-based approach is much more common, the remainder of this chapter concentrates on this traditional job analysis process.

USES OF JOB ANALYSIS

Effective HR management demands that job analysis be the foundation for a number of other HR activities.[1] The process of analyzing jobs in organizations requires planning of several factors. As Figure 4-1 indicates, some of the considerations are how it is to be done, who provides data, and who conducts the analysis and uses the data so that job descriptions and job specifications can be prepared and reviewed. Once those decisions are made, then several results are linked to a wide range of HR activities. The most fundamental use of job analysis is to provide the information necessary to develop job descriptions and specifications.

Job Descriptions and Job Specifications

In most cases, the job description and job specifications are combined into one document that contains several different sections. A brief overview of each section follows next; a more detailed discussion appears later in the chapter.

A **job description** indicates the tasks, duties, and responsibilities of a job. It identifies what is done, why it is done, where it is done, and—briefly—how it is done.

Performance standards should flow directly from a job description, telling what the job accomplishes and how performance is measured in key areas of the job description. If employees know what is expected and how performance is to be measured, they have a much better chance of performing satisfactorily.

FIGURE 4-1 Decisions in the Job Analysis Process

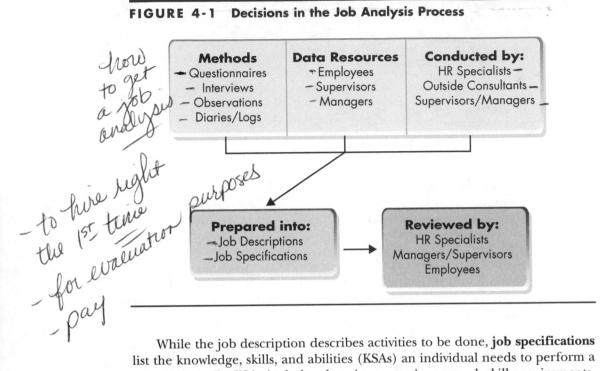

(handwritten notes in margin)
how to get a job analysis
— to hire right the 1st time
— for evaluation purposes
— pay

Methods
— Questionnaires
— Interviews
— Observations
— Diaries/Logs

Data Resources
— Employees
— Supervisors
— Managers

Conducted by:
HR Specialists
Outside Consultants
Supervisors/Managers

Prepared into:
— Job Descriptions
— Job Specifications

Reviewed by:
HR Specialists
Managers/Supervisors
Employees

While the job description describes activities to be done, **job specifications** list the knowledge, skills, and abilities (KSAs) an individual needs to perform a job satisfactorily. KSAs include education, experience, work skill requirements, personal abilities, and mental and physical requirements. It is important to note that accurate job specifications identify what KSAs a person needs to do the job, not necessarily what qualifications the current employee possesses.

Job Families and Organization Charts

Once all jobs in the organization have been identified, it is often helpful for communicating with employees to group the jobs into job families and display them on an organization chart. There are various ways of identifying and grouping job families. A **job family** is a grouping of jobs with similar characteristics. In identifying job families, significant emphasis is placed on measuring the similarity of jobs. An **organization chart** depicts the relationships among jobs in an organization. Organization charts have traditionally been hierarchical that show the reporting relationships for authority and responsibilities. In most organizations, the charts can help clarify who reports to whom.

Job Analysis and HR Activities

The completion of job descriptions and job specifications, based on job analysis, is at the heart of many other HR activities, as Figure 4-2 indicates. But even if legal requirements did not force employers to do job analysis, effective HR management would demand it.

FIGURE 4-2   Job Analysis and Other HR Activities

HR Planning. HR planning requires auditing of current jobs. Current job descriptions provide the basic details necessary for this internal assessment, including such items as the jobs available, current number of jobs and positions, and reporting relationships of the jobs. By identifying the functions currently being performed and calculating the time being spent to perform them, managers and HR specialists can redesign jobs to eliminate unnecessary tasks and combine responsibilities where desirable.

Recruiting and Selection. Equal employment opportunity guidelines clearly require a sound and comprehensive job analysis to validate recruiting and selection criteria. Without a systematic investigation of a job, an employer may be using requirements that are not specifically job related. Organizations use job analysis to identify job specifications in order to plan how and where to obtain employees for anticipated job openings, whether recruited internally or externally.

Compensation. Job analysis information is vital when determining compensation. As part of identifying appropriate compensation, job analysis information is used to determine job content for *internal* comparisons of responsibilities and *external* comparisons with the compensation paid by competing employers. Information from job analysis can be used to give more weight, and therefore more pay, to jobs involving more difficult tasks, duties, and responsibilities.

Training and Development. By defining what activities make up a job, a job analysis helps the supervisor explain that job to a new employee. Information from job descriptions and job specifications can also help in career planning by showing employees what is expected in jobs that they may choose in the future. Job specification information can point out areas in which employees might need to develop in order to further their careers.

Performance Appraisal. With performance standards to compare what an employee is supposed to be doing with what the person actually has done, a supervisor can determine the employee's performance level. The performance appraisal process should then tie to the job description and performance standards. Developing clear, realistic performance standards can also reduce communication problems in performance appraisal feedback among managers, supervisors, and employees.

Safety and Health. Job analysis information is useful in identifying possible job hazards and working conditions associated with jobs. From the information gathered, managers and HR specialists can work together to identify the health and safety equipment needed, specify work methods, and train workers.[2]

the hazards & working conditions

diciplinary action, etc.

Union Relations. Where workers are represented by a labor union, job analysis is used in several ways. First, job analysis information may be needed to determine whether the job should be covered by the union agreements. Second, it is common in unionized environments for job descriptions to be very specific about what tasks are and are not covered in a job. Finally, well-written and specific job descriptions can reduce the number of grievances filed by workers.

Job Analysis and Legal Issues

Permeating the discussion of equal employment laws, regulations, and court cases in preceding chapters is the concept that legal compliance must focus on the jobs that individuals perform. The 1978 Uniform Selection Guidelines make it clear that HR requirements must be tied to specific job-related factors if employers are to defend their actions as a business necessity.

The Americans with Disabilities Act (ADA). The Americans with Disabilities Act (ADA) has increased the emphasis on job analysis, job descriptions, and job specifications. HR managers and their organizations must identify job activities and then document the steps taken to identify job responsibilities. One result of the ADA is increased emphasis by employers on conducting job analysis, as well as developing and maintaining current and accurate job descriptions.[3] Having identified the essential job functions through a job analysis, an employer must be prepared to make reasonable accommodations. Again, the core job duties and KSAs must be considered.

Wage/Hours Regulations. Typically, a job analysis identifies the percentage of time spent on each duty in a job. This information helps determine whether someone should be classified as exempt or nonexempt under the wage/hour laws. These laws indicate that the percentage of time employees spend on routine, manual, or clerical duties affects whether they must be paid overtime for hours over forty per week.

Behavioral Aspects of Job Analysis

A detailed examination of jobs, while necessary, can be a demanding and threatening experience for both managers and employees, in part because job analysis can identify the difference between what is currently being performed in a job and what *should* be done. Job analysis involves determining what the "core" job is.

Employees and managers also tend to inflate the importance and significance of their jobs. Because job analysis information is used for compensation purposes, both managers and employees hope that "puffing up" their jobs will result in higher pay levels. Also, some employees may fear that an analysis of their jobs will put a "straitjacket" on them, limiting their creativity and flexibility by formalizing their duties. However, it does not necessarily follow that analyzing a job will limit job scope or depth. Having a well-written and well-communicated job description can assist employees by clarifying what their roles are and what is expected of them.[4] Perhaps the most effective way to handle anxieties is to involve the employees in the revision process.

JOB ANALYSIS METHODS

Job analysis information can be gathered in a variety of ways. Common methods are observation, interviews, questionnaires, and specialized methods of analysis. Combinations of these approaches frequently are used, depending on the situation and the organization.[5] Each of these methods is discussed in some detail next.

Observation

When the observation method is used, a manager, job analyst, or industrial engineer observes the individual performing the job and takes notes to describe the tasks and duties performed. Observation may be continuous or based on intermittent sampling. Use of the observation method is limited because many jobs do not have complete and easily observed job duties or complete job cycles. Thus, observation may be more useful for repetitive jobs and in conjunction with other methods.

Interviews

The interview method of gathering information requires that a manager or HR specialist visit each job site and talk with the employees performing each job. A standardized interview form is used most often to record the information. Frequently, both the employee and the employee's supervisor must be interviewed to obtain a complete understanding of the job. The interview method can be quite time-consuming, especially if the interviewer talks with two or three employees doing each job. Professional and managerial jobs often are more complicated to analyze and usually require longer interviews. For these reasons, combining the interview with one of the other methods is suggested.

Questionnaires

The questionnaire is a widely used method of gathering data on jobs. A survey instrument is developed and given to employees and managers to complete. The major advantage of the questionnaire method is that information on a large number of jobs can be collected inexpensively in a relatively short period of time. However, the questionnaire method assumes that employees can accurately analyze and communicate information about their jobs. Employees may vary in their perceptions of the jobs, and even in their literacy. For these reasons, the questionnaire method is usually combined with interviews and observations to clarify and verify the questionnaire information.

Computerized Job Analysis

As computer technology has expanded, researchers have developed computerized job analysis systems. An important feature of computerized job analysis sources is the specificity of data that can be gathered. All of this specific data is compiled into a job analysis database.

A computerized job analysis system often can reduce the time and effort involved in writing job descriptions. These systems have banks of job duty statements that relate to each of the task and scope statements of the questionnaires.

THE JOB ANALYSIS PROCESS

The process of job analysis must be conducted in a logical manner, following appropriate management and professional psychometric practices. Therefore, a multistage process usually is followed, regardless of the job analysis methods used. The stages for a typical job analysis are outlined here, but they may vary with the methods used and the number of jobs included. Figure 4-3 illustrates the basic stages of the process.

Planning

It is crucial that the job analysis process be planned before beginning the gathering of data from managers and employees. Probably the most important consideration is to identify the objectives of the job analysis. Maybe it is just to update job descriptions. Or, it may include as an outcome revising the compensation programs in the organization. Another objective could be to redesign the jobs in a department or division of the organization. Also, the objective could be

FIGURE 4-3   Stages in the Job Analysis Process

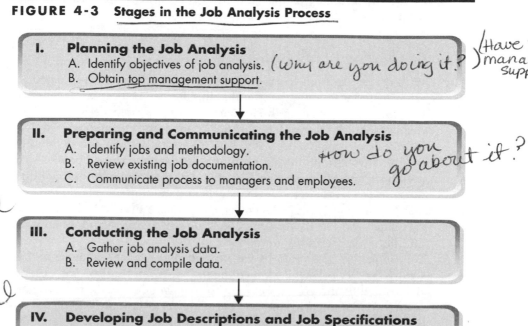

I.   Planning the Job Analysis
A. Identify objectives of job analysis. *(why are you doing it?)* *(Have Top management support)*
B. Obtain <u>top management</u> support.

II.   Preparing and Communicating the Job Analysis
A. Identify jobs and methodology.
B. Review existing job documentation.   *How do you go about it?*
C. Communicate process to managers and employees.

III.   Conducting the Job Analysis
A. Gather job analysis data.
B. Review and compile data.

IV.   Developing Job Descriptions and Job Specifications
A. Draft job descriptions and specifications.
B. Review drafts with managers and employees. *To approve & Agree*
C. Identify recommendations. —
D. Finalize job descriptions and recommendations.

V.   Maintaining and Updating Job Descriptions and Job Specifications
A. Update job descriptions and specifications as organization changes.
B. Periodically review all jobs.

you need review ...s on a annual basis

to change the structure in parts of the organization to align it better with business strategies.

Preparation and Introduction

Preparation consists of identifying the jobs under review. Another task in the identification phase is to review existing documentation. Existing job descriptions, organization charts, previous job analysis information, and other industry-related resources all may be useful to review. A crucial step is to communicate and explain the process to managers, affected employees, and other concerned people, such as union stewards. Explanations should address the natural concerns and anxieties people have when someone puts their jobs under close scrutiny and anticipate issues likely to arise.

Conducting the Job Analysis

With the preparation completed, the job analysis can be conducted. The methods selected will determine the timeline for the project. Sufficient time should be allotted for obtaining the information from employees and managers. Once details from job analysis have been compiled, they should be sorted by job family and organizational unit. This step allows for comparison of details from similar jobs throughout the organization. The data also should be reviewed for completeness, and follow-up may be needed in the form of additional interviews or questions to be answered by managers and employees.

At this stage, the job analysts will prepare draft job descriptions and job specifications. The drafts should be relatively complete and identify areas where additional clarifications are needed.

Generally, organizations have found that having managers and employees write job descriptions is not recommended. When finished, job descriptions are distributed by the HR department to managers, supervisors, and employees. It is important that each supervisor or manager review the completed description with individual employees so that there is understanding and agreement on the content that will be linked to performance appraisals, as well as to all other HR activities.

Once job descriptions and specifications have been completed and reviewed by all appropriate individuals, a system must be developed for keeping them current. Otherwise, the entire process, beginning with job analysis, may have to be repeated in several years.

JOB DESCRIPTIONS AND JOB SPECIFICATIONS

The output from analysis of a job is used to develop a job description and job specifications. Together, they summarize job analysis information in a readable format and provide the basis for defensible job-related actions. They also serve individual employees by providing documentation by management that identifies their jobs.

Job Description Components

A typical job description, such as the one in Appendix F, contains several major parts. Overviews of the most common components are presented next.

Identification. The first part of the job description is the identification section, in which the job title, reporting relationships, department, location, and date of analysis may be given. Usually, it is advisable to note other information that is useful in tracking jobs and employees through a human resource information system.

General Summary. The second part is the general summary which is a concise statement of the general responsibilities and components that make the job different from others. One HR specialist has characterized the general summary statement as follows: "In thirty words or less, describe the essence of the job."

Essential Functions and Duties. The third part of the typical job description lists the essential functions and duties. It contains clear, precise statements on the major tasks, duties, and responsibilities performed. Writing this section is the most time-consuming aspect of preparing job descriptions.

Job Specifications. The next portion of the job description gives the qualifications needed to perform the job satisfactorily. The job specifications typically are stated as (1) knowledge, skills, and abilities, (2) education and experience, and (3) physical requirements and/or working conditions. The components of the job specifications provide information necessary to determine what accommodations might and might not be possible under Americans with Disabilities Act regulations.

Disclaimer and Approvals. The final section on many job descriptions contains approval signatures by appropriate managers and a legal disclaimer. This disclaimer allows employers to change employees' job duties or request employees to perform duties not listed, so that the job description is not viewed as a "contract" between the employer and the employee.

Writing Job Descriptions

The ADA focused attention on the importance of well-written job descriptions. Legal compliance requires that they accurately represent the actual jobs. Job titles should be descriptive of job functions performed. The general format for an essential function statement is as follows: (1) *action verb*, (2) *to what applied*, (3) *what/how/how often*. There is a real art to writing statements that are sufficiently descriptive without being overly detailed. It is important to use precise action verbs that accurately describe the employee's tasks, duties, and responsibilities. The language of the ADA has stressed the importance of arranging job duties so that the most essential (in criticality and amount of time spent) be listed first and the supportive or marginal ones listed later. Within that framework, specific functional duties should be grouped and arranged in some logical pattern. If a job requires an accounting supervisor to prepare several reports, among other functions, statements relating to the preparation of reports should be grouped together. The *miscellaneous clause* typically listed last is included to assure some managerial flexibility.

Writing Job Specifications

Job specifications can be developed from a variety of information sources. Obviously, the job analysis process provides the primary starting point. But any KSA included must be based on what is really needed to perform a job. Furthermore, the job specifications listed should reflect what is necessary for satisfactory job performance, not what the ideal candidate would have.[6] In light of the ADA, it is crucial that the physical and mental dimensions of each job be clearly identified. If lifting, stooping, standing, walking, climbing, or crawling is required, it should be noted. Also, weights to be lifted should be specified, along with specific visual and hearing requirements of jobs.

NOTES

1. Institute for Job & Occupational Analysis Organization dedicated to research and application of job analysis and occupational analysis technologies and methods.
   http://www.ijoa.org
2. "Company Finds Job Analysis Key in Relieving Employee 'Discomfort,'" *Human Resources Report*, May 11, 1998, 501.
3. Kenneth H. Pritchard, "ADA Compliance: Job Analysis Is the Key," SHRM White Paper, 1998.
   http://www.shrm.org
4. PAQ Services
   Describes the Position Analysis Questionnaire and a database of jobs analyzed using the PAQ.
   http://www.paq.com
5. For more details on any of the methods discussed, see Robert D. Gatewood and Hubert S. Feild, *Human Resource Selection*, 4th ed. (New York: The Dryden Press, 1998), 324–369.
6. Edward L. Levine et al., "A Methodology for Developing and Validating Minimum Qualifications," *Personnel Psychology* 50, 1997, 1009–1023.

SUGGESTED READINGS

David D. Dubois, *The Competency Casebook*, HRD Press, 1998.

George T. Milkovich and Jerry M. Newman, *Compensation*, 6th ed., BPI-Irwin, 1999.

Roger J. Plachy and Sandra J. Plachy, *More Results-Oriented Job Descriptions*, AMACOM, 1998.

U.S. Department of Labor, *Dictionary of Occupational Titles*, U.S. Government Printing Office, 1991.

SUGGESTED INTERNET RESOURCES

CMQ Job Analysis. Discusses research on job analysis, specifically task-based methods.
http://harvey.psyc.vt.edu

Job Analysis Internet Guide. Provides information on job analysis methods, legal issues, and processes.
http://www.hr-guide.com/jobanalysis.htm

CHAPTER 5

Staffing

Effective staffing helps minimize problems in an organization through recruiting and selecting qualified people using established criteria and predictors.

Staffing is the process of matching appropriate people with appropriate jobs. From the viewpoint of organizations, staffing entails using HR planning information to determine the correct numbers and kinds of candidates, locating them, and then selecting those who are most likely to be satisfactory employees. From the standpoint of job applicants, the staffing process affects how they see jobs and organizations, and the likelihood that they will be matched with jobs that are rewarding for them. Staffing consists of recruiting and selection.

Many employers currently are facing shortages of workers with the appropriate knowledge, skills, and abilities (KSAs) in tight labor markets. There actually is not one but several **labor markets** that are the external sources from which employers attract employees. There are many ways to identify labor markets, including by geographical area, type of skill, and educational level. Some labor market segments might include managerial, clerical, professional and technical, and blue-collar. Classified differently, some markets are local, others regional, others national; there are international labor markets as well. To understand labor markets in which recruiting takes place, one must consider three different concepts: *labor force population, applicant population,* and *applicant pool.*

The **labor force population** includes all individuals who are available for selection if all possible recruitment strategies are used. This vast array of possible applicants may be reached in very different ways.

The **applicant population** is a subset of the labor force population that is available for selection using a particular recruiting approach. At least four recruiting decisions affect the nature of the applicant population:

- ▶ *Recruiting method:* advertising media chosen
- ▶ *Recruiting message:* what is said about the job and how it is said
- ▶ *Applicant qualifications required:* education level and amount of experience necessary
- ▶ *Administrative procedures:* time of year recruiting is done, follow-ups with applicants, and use of previous applicant files

The **applicant pool** consists of all people who are actually evaluated for selection. The applicant pool at this step will depend on the reputation of the organization and industry as a place to work, the screening efforts of the organization, and the information available to the applicant population. Assuming a suitable candidate can be found, the final selection is made from the applicant pool.

The supply and demand of workers in the labor force population has a substantial impact on the staffing strategies of organizations. Internal labor markets also influence recruiting because many employers choose to promote from within whenever possible, and hire externally only for entry-level jobs. A discussion of these and other strategic decisions to be made in recruiting follows.

PLANNING AND STRATEGIC DECISIONS ABOUT RECRUITING

The decisions that are made about recruiting help dictate not only the types and numbers of applicants, but also how difficult or successful recruiting efforts may be. Figure 5-1 shows an overview of these recruiting decisions. **Recruiting** involves identifying where to recruit, whom to recruit, and what the job requirements will be. One key consideration is deciding about internal versus external searches that must be made.

Internal versus External Recruiting

Both advantages and disadvantages are associated with promoting from within the organization (internal recruitment) and hiring from outside the organization (external recruitment) to fill openings. Most organizations combine the use of internal and external methods. Organizations that operate in a rapidly changing environment and competitive conditions may need to place a heavier emphasis on external sources in addition to developing internal sources. However, for organizations existing in environments that change slowly, promotion from within may be more suitable.

Flexible Staffing

Decisions as to whom should be recruited hinge on whether to seek traditional full-time employees or use more flexible approaches. These approaches might include temporaries, independent contractors, or professional employer organizations (PEOs) and "leased" employees.

FIGURE 5-1   Recruiting Decisions

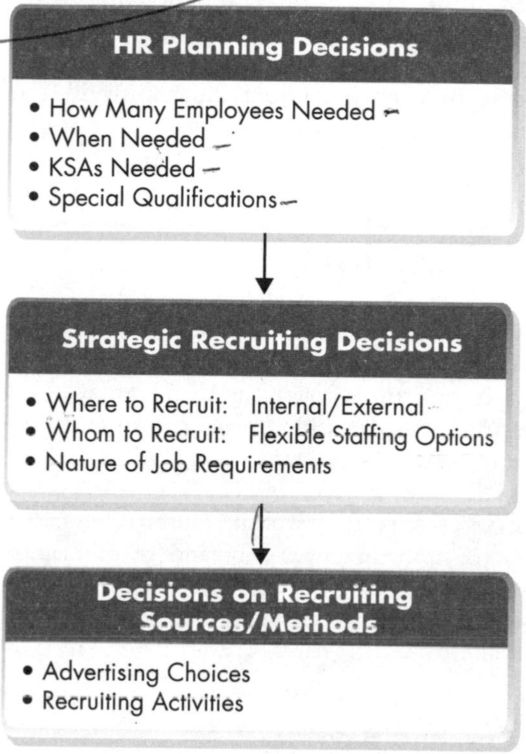

HR Planning Decisions

- How Many Employees Needed
- When Needed
- KSAs Needed
- Special Qualifications

↓

Strategic Recruiting Decisions

- Where to Recruit: Internal/External
- Whom to Recruit: Flexible Staffing Options
- Nature of Job Requirements

↓

Decisions on Recruiting Sources/Methods

- Advertising Choices
- Recruiting Activities

Employers that use **temporary employees** can hire their own temporary staff or use agencies supplying temporary workers on a rate-per-day or per-week basis. The use of temporary workers may make sense for an organization if its work is subject to seasonal or other fluctuations. Hiring regular employees to meet peak employment needs would require that the employer find some tasks to keep employees busy during less active periods or resort to layoffs.

Some firms employ independent contractors to perform specific services on a contract basis. However, those contractors must be independent as determined by the U.S. Internal Revenue Service and the U.S. Department of Labor.

Employee leasing is a concept that has grown rapidly in recent years. The employee leasing process is simple: An employer signs an agreement with an employee leasing company, after which the existing staff is hired by the leasing firm and leased back to the company. For a fee, a small-business owner or operator turns his or her staff over to the leasing company, which then writes the paychecks, pays the taxes, prepares and implements HR policies, and keeps all the required records.

The job can sometimes be changed specifically in order to alter the recruiting situation. A decision might be made to improve characteristics of vacant positions by raising salaries, increasing benefits, or redesigning the job for a different level of applicant. Also, jobs may be changed to reduce turnover and increase retention of employees, which means less need for recruiting and fewer empty jobs. Compensation is commonly used to improve retention, along with better opportunities for promotion and transfer, recognition, training, and benefits.

INTERNAL RECRUITING

Internal recruiting means focusing on current employees and others with previous contact with an employing organization. Friends of present employees, former employees, and previous applicants may be sources. Promotions, demotions, and transfers also can provide additional people for an organizational unit, if not for the entire organization.

Among the ways in which internal recruiting sources have an advantage over external sources is that they allow management to observe the candidate for promotion (or transfer) over a period of time and to evaluate that person's potential and specific job performance. Also, an organization that promotes its own employees to fill job openings may give those employees added motivation to do a good job.

Job Posting and Bidding

The major means for recruiting employees for other jobs within the organization is through **job posting and bidding,** whereby the employer provides notices of job openings and employees respond by applying for specific openings. The organization can notify employees of job vacancies by posting notices via e-mail, or in some other way inviting employees to apply for jobs. Job posting and bidding systems can be ineffective if handled improperly. Jobs generally are posted before any external recruiting is done. The organization must allow a reasonable period of time for present employees to check notices of available jobs before it considers external applicants.

Promotion and Transfer

Many organizations choose to fill vacancies through promotions or transfers from within whenever possible. Although most often successful, promotions from within have some drawbacks as well. The person's performance on one job may not be a good predictor of performance on another, because different skills may be required on the new job. Also, in most organizations promotions may not be an effective way to speed the movement of protected-class individuals up through the organization if that is an organizational concern.

Current Employee Referrals

A reliable source of people to fill vacancies is composed of friends and/or family members of current employees. Employees can acquaint potential applicants with the advantages of a job with the company, furnish letters of introduction, and encourage them to apply. These are external applicants recruited using an internal information source. Some employers pay employees incentives for referring individuals with specialized skills that are difficult to recruit through normal means.

Recruiting Former Employees and Applicants

Former employees and former applicants are also good internal sources for recruitment. In both cases, there is a time-saving advantage, because something is already known about the potential employee.

Internal Recruiting Database

Computerized internal talent banks, or applicant tracking systems, can be used to furnish a listing of the KSAs available for organizations. Employers that must deal with a large number of applications and job openings have found it beneficial to use such software as part of a human resource information system.

EXTERNAL RECRUITING

If internal sources do not produce enough acceptable candidates for jobs, many external sources are available. These sources include schools, colleges and universities, media sources, trade and competitive sources, employment agencies, executive search firms, and the Internet.

Schools

High schools or vocational/technical schools may be a good source of new employees for many organizations. A successful recruiting program with these institutions is the result of careful analysis and continual contact with individual schools.

Colleges and Universities

At the college or university level, the recruitment of graduating students is a large-scale operation for many organizations. Most colleges and universities maintain placement offices in which employers and applicants can meet.

Media Sources

Media sources such as newspapers, magazines, television, radio, and billboards are widely used. Whatever medium is used, it should be tied to the relevant labor market and provide sufficient information on the company and the job. When using recruitment advertisements in the media, employers should ask five key questions:

▶ What is the ad suppose to accomplish?

▶ Who are the people we want to reach?

▶ What should the advertising message convey?

▶ How should the message be presented?

▶ Where should it be placed?

Trade and Competitive Sources

Other sources for recruiting are *professional and trade associations, trade publications,* and *competitors.* Many professional societies and trade associations publish newsletters or magazines containing job ads. Such publications may be a good source of specialized professionals needed in an industry.

Employment Agencies

Every state in the United States has its own state-sponsored employment agency. These agencies operate branch offices in many cities throughout the state and do not charge fees to applicants or employers.

Private employment agencies are also found in most cities. For a fee collected from either the employee or the employer, usually the employer, these agencies do some preliminary screening for an organization and put the organization in touch with applicants.

Executive Search Firms

Some employment agencies focus their efforts on executive, managerial, and professional positions. These executive search firms are split into two groups: (1) contingency firms that charge a fee only after a candidate has been hired by a client company, and (2) retainer firms that charge a client a set fee whether or not the contracted search is successful. Most of the larger firms work on a retainer basis.

Internet Recruiting

Organizations first started using computers as a recruiting tool by advertising jobs on a *bulletin board service,* from which prospective applicants would contact the company. Then some companies began to take e-mail applications. Now many employers are not only posting jobs and accepting résumés and cover letters online, but also are conducting employment interviews online.

[handwritten margin note: 5 key questions employers should ask when using media sources]

RECRUITING EVALUATION

Evaluating the success of recruiting efforts is important. General areas for evaluating recruiting include the following:

- ▶ *Quantity of applicants:* Because the goal of a good recruiting program is to generate a large pool of applicants from which to choose, quantity must be sufficient to fill job vacancies.
- ▶ *EEO goals met:* The recruiting program is the key activity used to meet goals for hiring protected-class individuals. This is especially relevant when a company is engaged in affirmative action to meet such goals.
- ▶ *Quality of applicants:* There is the issue of whether the qualifications of the applicant pool are sufficient to fill the job openings, whereby the applicants meet job specifications and perform the jobs.
- ▶ *Cost per applicant hired:* Cost varies depending on the position being filled, but knowing how much it costs to fill an empty position puts turnover and salary levels in perspective.
- ▶ *Time required to fill openings:* The length of time it takes to fill openings is another means of evaluating recruiting efforts. If openings are filled quickly with qualified candidates, the work and productivity of the organization are not delayed by vacancies.

In summary, the effectiveness of various recruiting sources will vary depending on the nature of the job being filled and the time available to fill it. But unless calculated, the effectiveness may not be entirely obvious.

NATURE OF SELECTION

→ choosing qualified individuals

Selection is the process of choosing qualified individuals who have relevant qualifications to fill jobs in an organization. Without qualified employees, an organization is in a poorer position to succeed. Selection is much more than just choosing the best available person. Selecting the appropriate set of KSAs—which come packaged in a human being—is an attempt to get a "fit" between what the applicant can do and wants to do, and what the organization needs.[1] Fit between the applicant and the organization affects both the employer's willingness to make a job offer and an applicant's willingness to accept a job. Fitting a person to the right job is called **placement**. More than anything else, placement of human resources should be seen as a *matching process*. Whether an employer uses specific KSAs or the more general approach, effective selection of employees involves using *criteria* and *predictors* of job performance.

fitting right person into the job.

Criteria, Predictors, and Job Performance

At the heart of an effective selection system is knowledge of what constitutes appropriate job performance and what characteristics in employees are associ-

FIGURE 5-2 **Job Performance, Selection Criteria, and Predictors**

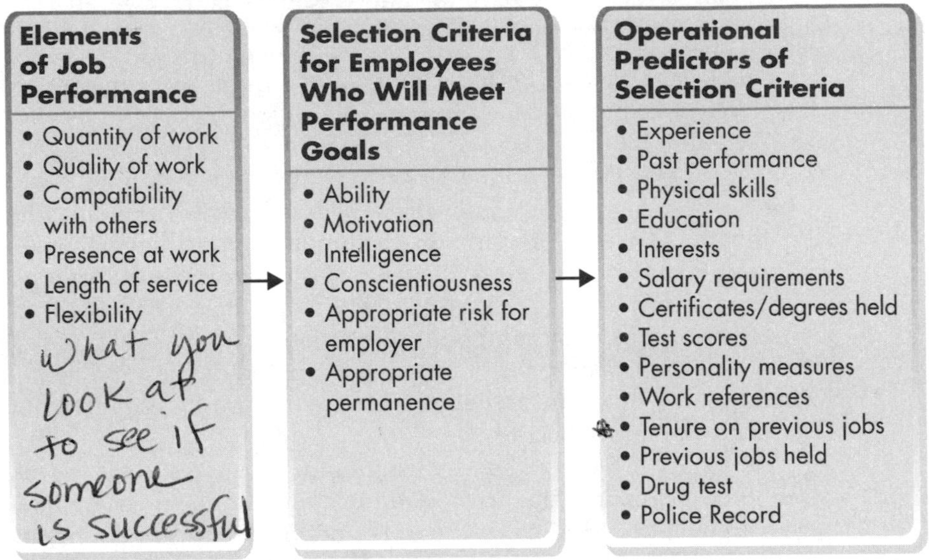

Elements of Job Performance	Selection Criteria for Employees Who Will Meet Performance Goals	Operational Predictors of Selection Criteria
• Quantity of work • Quality of work • Compatibility with others • Presence at work • Length of service • Flexibility	• Ability • Motivation • Intelligence • Conscientiousness • Appropriate risk for employer • Appropriate permanence	• Experience • Past performance • Physical skills • Education • Interests • Salary requirements • Certificates/degrees held • Test scores • Personality measures • Work references • Tenure on previous jobs • Previous jobs held • Drug test • Police Record

[handwritten: what you look at to see if someone is successful]

ated with that performance.[2] Once the definition of employee success (performance) is known, the employee specifications required to achieve that success can be determined. A **selection criterion** is a characteristic that a person must have to do the job successfully. Figure 5-2 shows that ability, motivation, intelligence, conscientiousness, appropriate risk, and permanence might be good selection criteria for many jobs. To predict whether a selection criterion (such as motivation or ability) is present, employers try to identify **predictors** as identifiable indicators of the selection criteria.

Legal Concerns

Generally, employers use a variety of pre-employment steps and predictors to ensure that applicants will fit available jobs. Selection is subject to all EEO concerns. It is increasingly important for employers to define carefully exactly who is an applicant, given the legal issues involved. If there is no written policy defining conditions that make a person an applicant, any people who call or send unsolicited résumés might later claim they were not hired because of illegal discrimination. A policy defining *applicant* might include the following aspects:

[handwritten: defining who they're considering for the job.]

▶ Applications are accepted only when there is an opening.
▶ Only individuals filling out application blanks are considered applicants.
▶ A person's application ceases to be effective after a designated date.
▶ Only a certain number of applications will be accepted.
▶ People must apply for specific jobs, not "any job."

[handwritten: → protects the business]

Selection Responsibilities

Organizations vary in how they allocate selection responsibilities between HR specialists and managers. Selection duties may be centralized into a specialized organizational unit that is part of an HR department. In smaller organizations, especially those with fewer than 100 employees, a full-time employment specialist or unit may be impractical.

THE SELECTION PROCESS — *depends on company, the person*

Most organizations take certain common steps to process applicants for jobs. Variations on this basic process depend on organizational size, nature of jobs to be filled, number of people to be selected, and pressure of outside forces. The selection process shown in Figure 5-3 is typical in a large organization.

Reception and Job Preview/Interest Screening

In addition to matching qualified people to jobs, the selection process has an important public-relations dimension. Discriminatory hiring practices, impolite interviewers, unnecessarily long waits, inappropriate testing procedures, and lack of follow-up letters can produce unfavorable impressions of an employer. In some cases, it is appropriate to have a brief interview, called an *initial screening* or a *job preview/interest screen,* to see if the applicant is likely to match any jobs available in the organization before allowing the individual to fill out an application form. The job preview/interest screen also can be done effectively by computer. Computerized processing of applicants can occur on several different levels. Computers can search résumés or application blanks for key words. Hundreds of large companies use types of artificial-intelligence (AI) or "text searching" software to scan, score, and track résumés of applicants. A second means of computerizing screening is conducting initial screening interviews electronically. Computer-assisted interviewing techniques can use tools such as videotaped scenarios to which applicants react.[3]

The purpose of a **realistic job preview (RJP)** is to inform job candidates of the "organizational realities" of a job so that they can more accurately evaluate their own job expectations. By presenting applicants with a clear picture of the job, the organization hopes to reduce unrealistic expectations, thereby reducing employee disenchantment and ultimately employee dissatisfaction and turnover. A review on research on RJPs found that they tend to result in applicants having lower job expectations.[4]

Application Forms

Application forms are widely used. Properly prepared, an application form serves four purposes:

FIGURE 5-3 **Selection Process Flowchart**

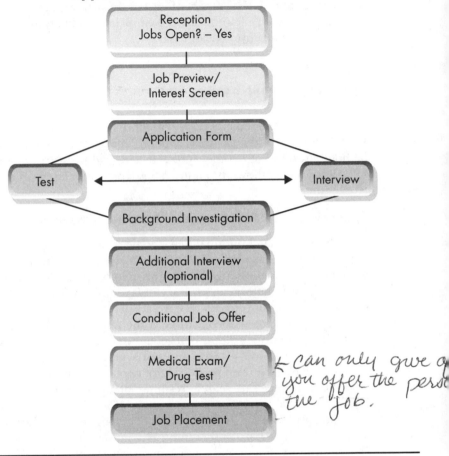

⟵ can only give a[s] you offer the pers[on] the job.

- ▶ It is a record of the applicant's desire to obtain a position.
- ▶ It provides the interviewer with a profile of the applicant that can be used in the interview.
- ▶ It is a basic employee record for applicants who are hired.
- ▶ It can be used for research on the effectiveness of the selection process.

Weighted Application Forms. One way employees can make the application form more job related is by developing a *weighted form.* A job analysis is used to determine the KSAs needed for the job, and an application form is developed to include items related to the selection criteria. Then weights, or numeric values, are placed on possible responses to the items based on their predictive value. The responses of applicants can be scored, totaled, and compared. Using weighted forms enables an employer to evaluate and numerically compare applicants' responses to a valid, job-related set of inquiries using computerized scoring.

Résumés. One of the most common methods applicants use to provide background information is the résumé. Technically, a résumé used in place of an application form must be treated by an employer as an application for EEO purposes.

Immigration/Citizenship Verification. The Immigration Reform and Control Act (IRCA) of 1986, as revised in 1990, requires that within seventy-two hours of hiring, an employer must determine whether a job applicant is a U.S. citizen, registered alien, or illegal alien. Those not eligible to work in this country must not be hired. The I-9 form is used by employers to identify the status of potential employees.

Selection Testing

According to the Uniform Selection Guidelines issued by the EEOC, any employment requirement is a "test." Some employers purchase prepared tests, while other employers develop their own tests. Many people feel that formal tests can be of great benefit in the selection process when properly used and administered.

Interpreting test results is not always straightforward, even if the test is valid. Individuals trained in testing and test interpretation should be involved in establishing and maintaining a testing system. Furthermore, the role of tests in the overall selection process must be kept in perspective.

Ability and Aptitude Tests. **Ability tests** assess the skills that individuals have already learned. **Aptitude tests** measure general ability to learn or acquire a skill. The typing tests given at many firms to secretarial applicants are commonly used ability tests. Other widely used tests measure mechanical ability and manual dexterity.

Mental ability tests measure reasoning capabilities. Some of the abilities tested include spatial orientation, comprehension and retention span, and general and conceptual reasoning. The General Aptitude Test Battery (GATB) is a widely used test of this type.

Assessment Centers. An assessment center is not necessarily a place, but a series of evaluative exercises and tests used for selection and development. The assessment uses multiple exercises and multiple raters. In one assessment center, candidates go through a comprehensive interview, pencil-and-paper test, individual and group simulations, and work exercises. The candidates' performances are then evaluated by a panel of trained raters. It is crucial to any assessment center that the tests and exercises reflect the job content and types of problems faced on the jobs for which individuals are being screened.[5]

Predictive value (

Psychological/Personality Tests. Personality is a unique blend of individual characteristics that affect interaction with the environment and help define a person. Historically, predictive validity has tended to be lower for personality tests used as predictors of performance on the job. However, some studies have shown that carefully chosen personality tests that logically connect to work requirements can help predict the interpersonal aspects of job success.[6]

Polygraph and Honesty Testing. Several types of tests have been devised to assess honesty. These include polygraph tests and paper-and-pencil honesty tests. Both are controversial.

The theory behind the polygraph is that if a person answers incorrectly, the body's physiological responses will "reveal" the falsification through the polygraph's recording mechanisms. As a result of concerns, Congress passed the Employee Polygraph Protection Act. The act bars polygraph use for pre-employment screening purposes by most employers. However, federal, state, and local government agencies are exempt from the act. The act does allow employers to continue to use polygraphs as part of internal investigations of theft or losses.

Firms use honesty tests to help reduce losses due to employee theft. With pre-employment polygraph testing no longer allowed, a growing number of firms have turned to such tests. These firms believe that giving honesty tests not only helps them screen out potentially dishonest individuals, but also sends a message to applicants and employees alike that dishonesty will not be tolerated.

Honesty tests are valid as broad screening devices for organizations but may not be as good at predicting whether a single individual will steal. Also, the use of these tests can have a negative public relations impact on applicants. A final concern is that the types of questions asked may constitute invasion of individual privacy.

Selection Interviewing

A **selection interview** is designed to identify information on a candidate and clarify information from other sources. This in-depth interview is designed to integrate all the information from application forms, tests, and reference checks, so that a decision can be made. Because of the integration required and the desirability of face-to-face contact, the interview is the most important phase of the selection process in many situations. Conflicting information may have emerged from tests, application forms, and references. As a result, the interviewer must obtain as much pertinent information about the applicant as possible during the limited interview time and evaluate this information against job standards. Finally, a selection decision must be made, based on all of the information obtained in the preceding steps.

The interview is not an especially valid predictor of job performance, but it has high "face validity"—that is, it seems valid to employers and they like it. Virtually all employers are likely to hire individuals using interviews.

Structured Interview. The **structured interview** uses a set of standardized questions that are asked of all applicants. Every applicant is asked the same basic questions, so that comparisons among applicants can more easily be made. This type of interview allows an interviewer to prepare job-related questions in advance and then complete a standardized interviewee evaluation form. Completion of such a form provides documentation if anyone, including an EEO enforcement body, should question why one applicant was selected over another.

Behavioral Description Interview. When responding to a **behavioral description interview,** applicants are required to give specific examples of how they have performed a certain procedure or handled a problem in the past. Like other structured methods, behavioral description interviews generally provide better validity than unstructured interviews.

Panel Interview. Usually, applicants are interviewed by one interviewer at a time. But when an interviewee must see several people, many of the interviews are redundant and therefore unnecessarily time-consuming. In a **panel interview**, several interviewers interview the candidate at the same time. All the interviewers hear the same responses. On the negative side, applicants are frequently uncomfortable with the group interview format.

BACKGROUND INVESTIGATION

Background investigation may take place either before or after the in-depth interview. It costs the organization some time and money, but it is generally well worth the effort. Unfortunately, some applicants misrepresent their qualifications and backgrounds. According to one survey of employers, the most common false data given are length of prior employment, past salary, criminal record, and former job title.[7]

Legal Constraints

Various federal and state laws have been passed to protect the rights of individuals whose backgrounds may be investigated during pre-employment screening. States vary in what they allow employers to investigate. For example, in some states, employers can request information from law enforcement agencies on any applicant. In some states, they are prohibited from getting certain credit information. Several states have passed laws providing legal immunity for employers who provide information on an employee to another employer.

Medical Examinations

The Americans with Disabilities Act prohibits a firm from rejecting an individual because of a disability. Also, the ADA prohibits asking job applicants any question relative to current or past medical history until a conditional job offer is made.

Drug Testing

Drug testing may be a part of a medical exam, or it may be done separately. Using drug testing as a part of the selection process has increased in the past few years, though not without controversy. Employers should remember that such tests are not infallible. The accuracy of drug tests varies according to the type of test used, the item tested, and the quality of the laboratory where the test samples are sent.

NOTES

1. John A. Parnell, "Improving the Fit between Organizations and Employees," *SAM Advanced Management Journal* 63, 1998, 35–42.
2. Kevin R. Murphy and Ann Harris Sharaella, "Implications of the Multidimensional Nature of Job Performance for the Validity of Selection Tests," *Personnel Psychology* 50, 1997, 823.
3. Linda Thornburg, "Computer-Assisted Interviewing Shortens the Hiring Cycle," *HR Magazine,* February 1998, 73.
4. Jean M. Phillips, "Effects of Realistic Job Previews on Multiple Organizational Outcomes," *Academy of Management Journal* 41, 1998, 673–690; and Peter W. Horn et al., "An Exploratory Investigation into Theoretical Mechanisms Underlying Realistic Job Previews," *Personnel Psychology* 51, 1998, 421.
5. Harold W. Goldstein et al., "The Role of Cognitive Ability in the Subgroup Differences and Incremental Validity of Assessment Center Exercises," *Personnel Psychology* 51, 1998, 357.
6. P.H. Raymark, Mark Schmidt, and Robert Guion, "Identifying Potentially Useful Personality Constructs for Employee Selection," *Personnel Psychology* 50, 1997, 723.
7. Sam Jensen and Mark Schorr, "Lying to Get a Job," *Nebraska Workplace Memo,* February 1999, 1.

SUGGESTED READINGS

Joan Brannick and Jim Harris, *Finding & Keeping Great Employees,* AMACOM, 1999.

Robert T. Gatewood and Hubert T. Feild, *Human Resource Selection,* 4th ed., Harcourt, 1999.

John McCarter and Ray Schreyer, *The Employer's Guide to Recruiting on the Internet,* Impact Publications, 1998.

N. Schmitt and D. Chan, *Personnel Selection,* Sage Publishers, 1998.

SUGGESTED INTERNET RESOURCES

Recruiters Network. Contains details on the Association for Internet Recruiting.
http://www.recruitersnetwork.com

America's Job Bank. Provides a job bank containing over two million job searchers and one million job listings.
http://www.ajb.dni.us

CHAPTER 6

Training and Development

Training and development are the means by which people learn their jobs. Effective orientation programs, understanding how learning occurs, and the way training and development are implemented make an impact on people's performance.

Training is a process whereby people acquire capabilities to aid in the achievement of organizational goals. Because this process is tied to a variety of organizational purposes, training can be viewed either narrowly or broadly. In a limited sense, training provides employees with specific, identifiable knowledge and skills for use on their present jobs. Sometimes a distinction is drawn between *training* and *development,* with development being broader in scope and focusing on individuals gaining *new* capabilities useful for both present and future jobs.

NATURE OF TRAINING

Training in organizations is offered in many different areas and different ways. Notice in Figure 6-1 that some of this training is conducted primarily in-house, whereas other types of training make greater use of external training resources.

Types of Internal Training

Training in on-the-job locations tends to be viewed as being very applicable to the job, it saves the cost of sending employees away for training, and it often avoids the cost of outside trainers. Often, technical training is conducted inside organizations. Technical training is usually skills-based—for example, training employees to run precision computer-controlled machinery. Due to rapid

FIGURE 6-1 Common Types of Training

- New employee orientation
- How to conduct performance appraisals
- Personal computer courses
- Team building

- Leadership training
- Sexual harassment training
- Hiring process
- Training the trainer
- Operating new equipment

[handwritten in margin: Training vs. development — utilizing the skills]

changes in technology, the building and updating of technical skills have become crucial.

External Training

External training may be used for several reasons:

▶ It may be less expensive for an employer to have an outside trainer conduct training in areas where internal training resources are limited.
▶ There may not be sufficient time to develop internal training materials.
▶ The HR staff may not have the level of expertise needed for the subject matter where training is needed.
▶ There are advantages to having employees interact with managers and peers in other companies in training programs held externally.

One growing trend is the *outsourcing* of training, in which vendors are used to train employees. For example, many software providers have users' conferences where employees from a number of companies receive detailed training on using the software and new features being added. Also, vendors can do training inside the organization if sufficient numbers of employees are to be trained.

Web-Based Training

The explosive growth of the Internet is changing how training is being done in organizations. As more and more employees use computers and have access to Internet portals, their employers are seeing the World Wide Web as a means for distributing training to employees who are located in widely diverse locations and jobs. It also should be recognized that Web-based training might not be appropriate for certain types of training. For instance, leadership skill training or other behaviorally-focused training and development may be done better face-to-face using increased trainee interactions.

In summary, training using the Web is likely to continue replacing classroom instruction in some of the training done by employers. Thus, more training may become distance learning and available on demand.

LEARNING PRINCIPLES: THE PSYCHOLOGY OF LEARNING

Often, trainers or supervisors present information and assume that merely by presenting it they have ensured that it will be learned. But learning takes place only when information is received, understood, and internalized in such a way that some change or conscious effort has been made to use the information. Some major learning principles that guide training efforts follow.

Intention to Learn

People learn at different rates and are able to apply what they learn differently. *Ability* to learn must be accompanied by motivation, or *intention,* to learn. Motivation to learn is determined by answers to questions such as these: "How important is my job to me?" "How important is it that I learn that information?" "Will learning this help me in any way?" "What's in it for me?"

Whole Learning

It is usually better to give trainees an overall view of what they will be learning than to deal immediately with the specifics. This concept is referred to as *whole learning* or *Gestalt learning.* As applied to job training, this means that instructions should be divided into small elements *after* employees have had the opportunity to see how all the elements fit together.

Reinforcement

The concept of **reinforcement** is based on the *law of effect,* which states that people tend to repeat responses that give them some type of positive reward and avoid actions associated with negative consequences. The reinforcers that an individual receives can be either external or internal, and many training situations provide both kinds.

Behavior Modification

A comprehensive approach to training has been developed based on the concept of reinforcement. This popular approach, *behavior modification,* uses the theories of psychologist B. F. Skinner, who asserted that "learning is not doing; it is changing what we do." Behavior modification makes use of four means of changing behavior, labeled *intervention* strategies. The four strategies are positive reinforcement, negative reinforcement, punishment, and extinction.

Immediate Confirmation

Another learning concept is **immediate confirmation**—people learn best if reinforcement is given soon after training. Feedback on whether a learner's response was right or wrong should be given as soon as possible after the response.

Learning Practice

Learning new skills requires practice and application of what is learned. Both research and experience show that when designing skill training, repetition, and practice are important considerations.

Behavior Modeling. The most elementary way in which people learn—and one of the best—is **behavior modeling**, or copying someone else's behavior. A variation of modeling occurs when people avoid making mistakes they see others make. The use of behavior modeling is particularly appropriate for skill training in which the trainees must use both knowledge and practice.

Active Practice. **Active practice** occurs when trainees perform job-related tasks and duties during training. It is more effective than simply reading or passively listening. Active practice can be structured in two ways. The first, **spaced practice**, occurs when several practice sessions are spaced over a period of hours or days. The other, **massed practice**, occurs when a person does all of the practice at once.

Transfer of Training

For effective *transfer of training* from the classroom to the job, two conditions must be met. First, trainees must be able to take the material learned in training and apply it to the job context in which they work. Second, use of the learned material must be maintained over time on the job.

ORIENTATION: TRAINING FOR NEW EMPLOYEES

Orientation is the planned introduction of new employees to their jobs, their co-workers, and the organization. However, orientation should not be a mechanical, one-way process. Because all employees are different, orientation must incorporate a sensitive awareness of the anxieties, uncertainties, and needs of the new employees. Orientation in one form or another is offered by most employers. Orientation requires cooperation between individuals in the HR unit and other managers and supervisors. The overall goal of orientation is to help new employees learn about the organization as soon as possible, so that they can begin contributing.

Both employers and new employees want individuals starting jobs to become as productive as possible relatively quickly. One facet of orientation that affects productivity is training new employees on the proper ways to perform their jobs. Some employers have experienced significant turnover of newly hired employees, and it is common for more than half of all new hires in hourly jobs to leave within their first year of employment. But employers with effective orientation programs have found that new employees stay longer.[1]

Organizational Overview

Another purpose of orientation is to inform new employees about the nature of the organization. A general organizational overview might include a brief review of the organization; the history, structure, key executives, purpose, products, and services of the organization; how the employee's job fits into the big picture; and other general information.

Another purpose of orientation is to ease the employee's entry into the work group. New employees often are concerned about meeting the people in their work units. Further, the expectations of the work group do not always parallel those presented at management's formal orientation. Also, if a well-planned formal orientation is lacking, the new employee may be oriented solely by the group of existing employees, possibly in ways not beneficial to the organization.

Establishing an Effective Orientation System

A systematic approach to orientation requires attention to attitudes, behaviors, and information that new employees need. Unfortunately, too often orientation is conducted rather haphazardly. The major components of an effective orientation system are preparing for new employees, providing them with needed information, presenting orientation information effectively, and conducting evaluation and follow-up on the initial orientation.

SYSTEMS APPROACH TO TRAINING

The success of orientation or any other type of training can be gauged by the amount of learning that occurs and is transferred to the job. But without a well-designed, systematic approach to training, what is learned may not be what is best for the organization. Figure 6-2 shows the relevant components of the three major phases in a training system.

Training Needs Assessment

Training is designed to help the organization accomplish its objectives. Determining organizational training needs is the diagnostic phase of setting training objectives. The first way to diagnose training needs is through organizational analysis, which considers the organization as a system. An important part of the company's strategic human resource planning is the identification of the KSAs that employers will need in the future as both jobs and organizations change.

FIGURE 6-2   Model of a Training System

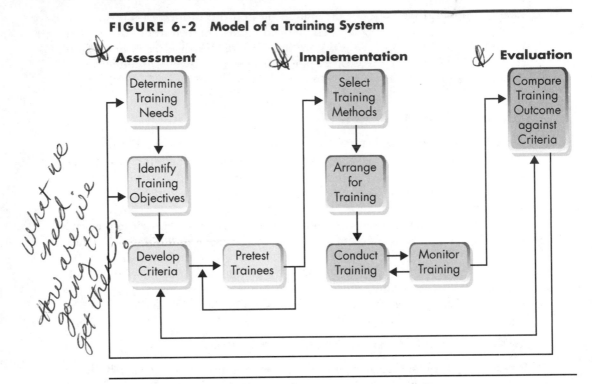

Specific sources of information and operational measures for an organizational-level needs analysis may include the following:

- ▶ Grievances
- ▶ Accident records
- ▶ Observations
- ▶ Exit interviews

- ▶ Complaints from customers
- ▶ Equipment utilization figures
- ▶ Training committee observations
- ▶ Waste/scrap/quality control data

The second way to diagnose training needs is through analyses of the tasks performed in the organization. To do these analyses, it is necessary to know the job requirements of the organization using job descriptions and job specifications that provide information on the required work.

The third means of diagnosing training needs focuses on individuals and how they perform their jobs. The use of performance appraisal data in making these individual analyses is the most common approach. In some instances, a good HR information system can be used to help identify individuals who require training in specific areas.

Once training needs have been identified using the various analyses, then training objectives and priorities must be established. All of the gathered data is used to compile a *gap analysis,* which identifies the distance between where an organization is with its employee capabilities and where it needs to be. Training objectives and priorities are set to close the gap.[2]

Implementing Training

Once training assessment has been done, the actual training can begin. Regardless of whether the training is job-specific or broader in nature, the appropriate training approach must be chosen. The following overview of common training approaches and techniques classifies them into several major groups.

On-the-Job Training (OJT). The most common type of training at all levels in an organization is *on-the-job training* (OJT). Whether or not the training is planned, people do learn from their job experiences, particularly if these experiences change over time. On-the-job training usually is done by the manager, other employees, or both. A manager or supervisor who trains an employee must be able to teach, and show, the employee what to do.

Simulation. Simulation is a training approach that uses a training site set up to be identical to the work site. In this setting, trainees can learn under realistic conditions but be away from the pressures of the production schedule. Behavioral simulations and computer-generated virtual reality have grown as computer technology and use of the Internet for training have grown. Virtual reality uses three-dimensional environments to replicate a job, using computers, audio equipment, and video equipment.

Behaviorally Experienced Training. Some training efforts focus on emotional and behavioral learning. **Behaviorally experienced training** focuses less on physical skills than on attitudes, perceptions, and interpersonal issues. There are several different types of behaviorally experienced training. Employees can learn about behavior by *role playing,* in which individuals assume identities in a certain situation and act them out. *Business games, case studies,* other cases called *incidents,* and short work assignments called *in-baskets* are other behaviorally experienced learning methods.

Classroom and Conference Training. Training seminars, courses, and presentations can be used in both skills-related and developmental training. Lectures and discussions are a major part of this training. The numerous management development courses offered by trade associations and educational institutions are examples of conference training.

Several aids are available to trainers presenting information. The most common are audio-visual aids and computer-assisted instruction. Another is distance training and learning using interactive two-way television or computer technology. Also, the growth of Web-based training and organizational intranets has grown.

Computer-Assisted Instruction. Through computer-assisted instruction (CAI) trainees learn by interacting with a computer. Application of CAI technology is driven by the need to improve the efficiency or effectiveness of a training situation and to enhance the transfer of learning to improve job performance. Computers lend themselves well to instruction, testing, drill and practice, and application through simulation. Training programs are becoming increasingly high-tech. Interactive media such as computers can take the place of more expensive instructor-led classroom training. The advancement in computer technology also has led to placing training programs on CD-ROMs which are distributed to trainees.

Evaluation of Training

Evaluation of training compares the post-training results to the objectives expected by managers, trainers, and trainees. Too often, training is done without any thought of measuring and evaluating it later to see how well it worked. Because training is both time-consuming and costly, evaluation should be done. Rather than doing training evaluation internally, some organizations are using **benchmark measures** of training that are compared from one organization to others. To do benchmarking, HR professionals in an organization gather data on training and compare it to data on training at other organizations in the industry and of their size.

[handwritten: use questionnaire]

HUMAN RESOURCE DEVELOPMENT

Development can be thought of as growing capabilities that go beyond those required by the current job; it represents efforts to improve employees' ability to handle a variety of assignments. Development is beneficial to both the organization and the individuals.

[handwritten: Training - (new employees)]

[handwritten: development - your growth (existing employees)]

At the organizational level, executives responsible for crafting the broader organizational strategies should establish a system for developing the people who will manage and achieve those identified strategies. The successful CEO is likely to have employee and managerial succession plans on several different succession "pathways" as part of that development.[3]

Merger and acquisition activities, and layoffs for other reasons, have changed the way people and organizations look at careers and development. The "new career" is one in which the individual—not the organization—manages his or her own development. Such self-development consists of the person's educational experiences, training, organizational experiences, projects, and even changes in occupational fields. Under this system, the individual's definition of success is a personal definition, not necessarily the organizational view.

Exactly what kind of development a given individual might need to expand his or her capabilities depends on both the person and the capabilities needed. However, the following are some important and common management capabilities to be developed:

▶ Action orientation
▶ Quality decisions
▶ Ethical values
▶ Technical skills

FIGURE 6-3   The HR Development Process in an Organization

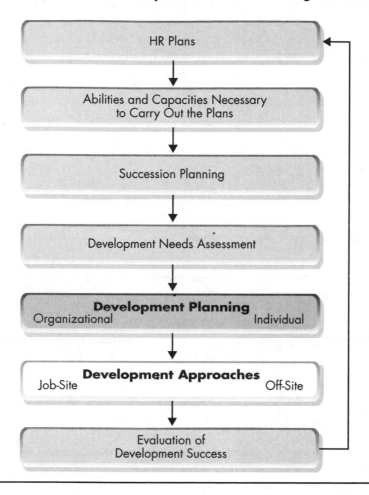

Equally important but much less commonly developed capabilities for successful managers are team building, developing subordinates, directing others, and dealing with uncertainty.

The HR Development Process

Development should begin with the HR plans of an organization that deal with analyzing, forecasting, and identifying the organizational needs for human resources. Also, HR planning allows anticipating the movement of people through the organization due to retirement, promotion, and transfers. It helps identify the capabilities that will be needed by the organization in the future and the development necessary to have people with those abilities on hand when needed. Figure 6-3 illustrates the HR development process.

Succession Planning

Succession planning can be an important part of development. For example, combined with skills training, management development, and promotion from within, it has been linked in one case to "turning around" a plant acquired by another company. The general result for the plant was a large increase in capacity over four years, with virtually no infusion of new managers or employees. Existing talent was developed instead. Succession planning can be especially important in small and medium-sized firms, but studies show that these firms have done the least planning. Few small and medium-sized firms have formal succession plans.

Replacement charts can be part of the development planning process by specifying the nature of development each employee needs in order to be prepared for the identified promotions. This information can be used to identify development needs and "promotion ladders" for people.

[handwritten note: succession planning — from one position to another]

Development Approaches

A number of job-site development methods are available. A major difficulty with development that takes place on the job site is that too often, unplanned activities are regarded as development. It is imperative that managers plan and coordinate development efforts so that desired development actually occurs.

Coaching. The oldest on-the-job development technique is coaching, which is the daily training and feedback given to employees by immediate supervisors. Coaching involves a continual process of learning by doing. For effective coaching, a healthy and open relationship must exist between employees and their supervisors or managers. Many firms conduct formal training courses to improve the coaching skills of their managers.

Job Rotation. **Job rotation** is widely used as a development technique. For example, a promising young manager may spend three months in the plant, three months in corporate planning, and three months in purchasing. When properly handled, such job rotation fosters a greater understanding of the organization.

Classroom Courses and Degrees. Many off-the-job development programs include some classroom instruction. The advantage of classroom training is that it is widely accepted because most people are familiar with it. But a disadvantage of classroom instruction is the lecture system, which encourages passive listening and reduced learner participation. Sometimes trainees have little opportunity to question, clarify, and discuss the lecture material. The effectiveness of classroom instruction depends on the group size, ability, instructor, and subject matter.

Management Development

Development is important for all employees, but especially so for managers. Unless managers are appropriately developed, resources (including employees) throughout the organization may not be managed well. Management development should be seen as a way of enhancing the knowledge and judgment needed by managers to meet the strategic objectives of the organization. Among these skills are leading, dealing with change, coaching and advising subordinates, controlling operations, and providing feedback.

Managerial Modeling. Managers, like other employees, learn by *behavior modeling,* or copying someone else's behavior. This is not surprising, because a great deal of human behavior is learned by modeling. Management development efforts can take advantage of natural human behavior by matching young or developing managers with appropriate models and then reinforcing the desirable behaviors exhibited.

Mentoring. **Mentoring** is a relationship in which managers at the midpoints in their careers aid individuals in the earlier stages of their careers. Technical, interpersonal, and political skills can be conveyed in such a relationship from the older to the younger person. Not only does the younger one benefit, but the older one may enjoy the challenge of sharing his or her wisdom. Most of the management development problems in the United States have resulted from inadequate HR planning and a lack of coordination of HR development efforts. Common problems include the following:

- ▸ Inadequate needs analysis
- ▸ Trying out fad programs or training methods
- ▸ Abdicating responsibility for development to staff
- ▸ Trying to substitute training for selection
- ▸ Lack of training among those who lead the development activities
- ▸ Using only "courses" as the road to development

CAREERS

People pursue careers to satisfy deeply individual needs. At one time, identifying with one employer seemed to fulfill many of those needs. Now, the distinction between the individual's career as the organization sees it and the career as the individual sees it is very important.

Organization-Centered vs. Individual-Centered Career Planning

Career planning can be somewhat confusing, because these two different perspectives exist. Career planning can be: (1) organization-centered; (2) individual-centered; or (3) both.

Organization-centered career planning focuses on jobs and on constructing career paths that provide for the logical progression of people between jobs in an organization. Individuals can follow these paths to advance in certain organizational units.

FIGURE 6-4 **Organizational and Individual Career-Planning Perspectives**

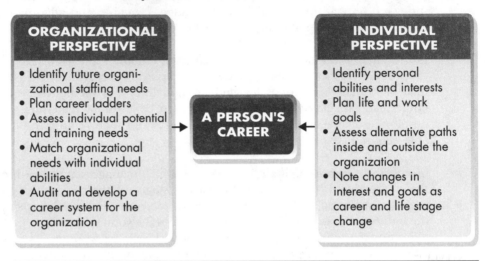

Individual-centered career planning focuses on individuals' careers rather than on organizational needs. It is done by employees themselves, and individual goals and skills are the focus of the analysis. Such analyses might consider situations both inside and outside the organization that could expand a person's career. Figure 6-4 shows the different perspectives.

Dual Career Paths for Technical and Professional Workers

Technical and professional workers, such as engineers and scientists, present a special challenge for organizations. Many of them want to stay in their labs or at their drawing boards rather than move into management; yet advancement frequently *requires* a move into management. Most of these people like the idea of the responsibility and opportunity associated with advancement, but they do not want to leave the technical puzzles and problems at which they excel. Therefore a technical career path is developed, whereby the individuals can progress to senior-level technical jobs without having to move into management.

Dual-Career Couples

It is important that the career development problems of dual-career couples be recognized as early as possible, especially if they involve transfer, so that realistic alternatives can be explored. Early planning by employees and their supervisors can prevent crisis. Whenever possible, having both partners involved, even when one is not employed by the company, has been found to enhance the success of such efforts. Recruiting a member of a dual-career couple increasingly means having an equally attractive job available for the candidate's partner at the new location. Dual-career couples have more to lose when relocating, and as a result often exhibit higher expectations and request more help and money in such situations.

Retirement

Whether retirement comes at age 50 or age 70, it can require a major adjustment for many people. Of course, from the standpoint of the organization, retirement is an orderly way to move people out at the ends of their careers. However, mindful of the problems that retirement poses for individuals, some organizations are experimenting with *phased retirement* through gradually reduced work weeks and increased vacation time. These and other preretirement and postretirement programs aimed at helping employees deal with problems aid in the transition.

NOTES

1. Rebecca Ganzel, "Putting Out the Welcome Mat," *Training*, March 1998, 54–61.
2. Paul Elliott, "Assessment Phase: Building Models and Defining Gaps," in Dana Gaines Robinson and James C. Robinson, eds., *Moving from Training to Performance* (San Francisco: Berrett-Koehler Publishers, Inc., 1998), 63–93.
3. Hugh P. Gunz et al., "New Strategy, Wrong Managers? What You Need to Know about Career Streams," *Academy of Management Executive*, May 1998, 21.

SUGGESTED READINGS

P. Nick Blanchard and James W. Thacker, *Effective Training: Systems, Strategies, and Practices*, Prentice-Hall, 1999.

Gerry Crispin and Mark Mehler, *Career X Roads*, MMC Group, 2000.

William K. Horton, *Designing Web-Based Training*, John Wiley & Sons, 2000.

Donald L. Kirkpatrick, *Evaluating Training Programs: The Four Levels*, Berret-Koehler, 1998.

Patricia Philips and Mel Silberman, *The 2000 Team and Organization Development Sourcebook*, McGraw-Hill, 1999.

SUGGESTED INTERNET RESOURCES

American Society for Training and Development. Describes training trends and issues, as well as the activities and programs of the ASTD.
http://www.astd.org

The Training Registry. Contains a directory of training courses, products, materials, and other resources.
http://www.trainingregistry.com

CHAPTER 7

Managing and Appraising Performance

Identifying and measuring employee performance is crucial to management of the organization. Employee performance is evaluated and communicated through performance appraisals.

Employees' job performance is an important issue for all employers. However, satisfactory performance does not happen automatically. It is more likely with a good performance management system. A **performance management system** consists of the processes used to identify, encourage, measure, evaluate, improve, and reward employee performance at work. In this chapter the focus is on *identifying, measuring,* and *evaluating* performance. Figure 7-1 shows performance management as part of the link between organizational strategy and results. The figure illustrates common performance management practices and outcomes.

IDENTIFYING AND MEASURING EMPLOYEE PERFORMANCE

Performance is essentially what an employee does or does not do. Employee performance that affects organizational performance could include the following:

- ▶ Quantity of output
- ▶ Quality of output
- ▶ Timeliness of output
- ▶ Presence at work
- ▶ Cooperativeness

FIGURE 7-1 **Linkage between Strategy, Outcomes, and Organizational Results**

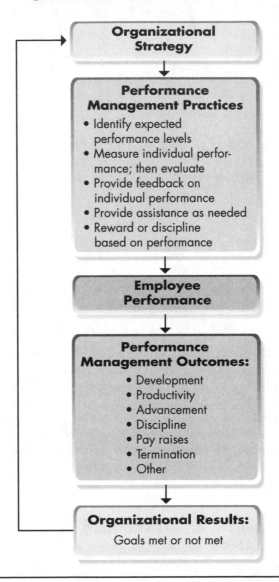

Obviously other dimensions of performance might be appropriate in certain jobs, but those listed are common to most. However, they are general; each job has specific **job criteria**, which are job performance dimensions that identify the elements most important in a job. For example, a college professor's job might include the job criteria of teaching, research, and service. In a sense, job criteria define what the organization is paying an employee to do. Because these criteria are important, individuals' performance on job criteria should be measured and compared against standards, and then the results be communicated to each employee.

In many jobs, multiple job criteria are the rule rather than the exception, and it follows that a given employee might be better at one job facet than another. Also, some criteria might have more importance than others to the organization. Weights are a way to show the relative importance of several job criteria in one job. In some universities a college professor's teaching might be a bigger part of the job than research or service, so that a weighting of the job criteria at a given university might look like this:

Job Criterion	Weight
Teaching	60%
Research	30%
Service	10%
Total	100%

Job Criteria and Information Types

The information that managers receive on how well employees are performing their jobs can be of three different types. *Trait-based* information identifies a subjective character trait—such as "pleasant personality," "initiative," or "creativity"—and may have little to do with the specific job. Traits tend to be ambiguous, and many court decisions have held that performance evaluations based on traits such as "adaptability" and "general demeanor" are too vague to use as the basis for performance-based HR decisions.

Behavior-based information focuses on specific behaviors that lead to job success. For a salesperson, the behavior of "verbal persuasion" can be observed and used as information on performance. Behavioral information is more difficult to identify, but has the advantage of clearly specifying the behaviors management wants to see. A potential problem is that there may be several behaviors, all of which can be successful in a given situation.

Results-based information considers what the employee has done or accomplished. For jobs in which measurement is straightforward, a results-based approach works very well. However, that which is measured tends to be emphasized, and the equally important but unmeasurable parts of the job may be left out. When measuring performance, it is important that relevant criteria be used. Generally, criteria are relevant when they focus on the most important aspects of employees' jobs. For example, measuring customer service representatives in an insurance claims center on their "appearance" may be less relevant than measuring the number of calls handled properly. This example stresses that the most important job criteria should be identified and be linked back to the employees' job descriptions.

Potential Criteria Problems

Because jobs usually include several duties and tasks, if the performance measures leave out some important job duties, the measures are *deficient.* For example, measuring the performance of an employment interviewer only on the number of applicants hired, but not on the quality of those hires, could be deficient. If irrelevant criteria are included, the criteria are said to be *contaminated.* An example of a contaminated criterion might be "appearance" for a telemarketing sales representative who is not seen by the customers. Managers use deficient or contaminated criteria for measuring performance much more often than they should.

Performance measures also can be thought of as *objective* or *subjective.* Objective measures can be directly counted—for example, the number of cars sold or the number of invoices processed. Subjective measures are more judgmental and more difficult to measure directly. One example of a subjective measure is a supervisor's ratings of an employee's customer service performance. Unlike subjective measures, objective measures tend to be more narrowly focused, which may lead to the objective measures being inadequately defined. However, subjective measures may be prone to contamination or other random errors. Neither is a panacea, and both should be used carefully.

Performance Standards

To know that an employee produces ten "units" per day does not provide a complete basis for judging employee performance as satisfactory or not. A *standard* against which to compare the information is necessary. Maybe fifteen units are considered a sufficient day's work. *Performance standards* define the expected levels of performance, and are "benchmarks," or "goals," or "targets"—depending on the approach taken. Realistic, measurable, clearly understood performance standards benefit both the organization and the employees. In a sense, performance standards define satisfactory job performance. It is important to establish standards before the work is performed, so that all involved will understand the level of accomplishment expected.

The extent to which standards have been met may be expressed in either numerical or verbal ratings—for example, "outstanding" or "unsatisfactory." It may sometimes be difficult for two or more people to reach agreement on exactly what the level of performance has been relative to the standard. Figure 7-2 shows terms used in evaluating employee performance on standards at one company. Notice that each level is defined in terms of performance standards, rather than numbers, in order to minimize different interpretations of the standards.

Standards are often set by someone external to the job, such as a supervisor or a quality control inspector, but they can be written effectively by employees as well. Experienced employees usually know what constitutes satisfactory performance of tasks in their job descriptions, and so do their supervisors.[1] Therefore, these individuals often can collaborate effectively on setting standards.

FIGURE 7-2   Terms Used to Define Standards at One Company

Outstanding. The person is so successful at this job criterion that special note should be made. Compared with the usual standards and the rest of the department, this performance ranks in the top 10%.

Very Good. Performance at this level is one of better-than-average performances in the unit, given the common standards and unit results.

Satisfactory. Performance is at or above the minimum standards. This level of performance is what one would expect from most experienced, competent employees.

Marginal. Performance is somewhat below the minimum-level standard on this job dimension. However, there appears to be potential to improve the rating within a reasonable time frame.

Unsatisfactory. Performance on this item in the job is well below standard, and there is serious question as to whether the person can improve to meet minimum standards.

THE NATURE AND USES OF PERFORMANCE APPRAISAL

Performance appraisal is the process of evaluating how well employees perform their jobs when compared to a set of standards, and then communicating that information to those employees. Such appraisal also has been called *employee rating, employee evaluation, performance review, performance evaluation,* and *results appraisal.*

Performance appraisal has two general uses in organizations, and these roles often create potential conflicts. One role is to measure performance for the purpose of rewarding or otherwise making administrative decisions about employees. Promotions or layoffs might hinge on these ratings, often making them more difficult for managers to do. Another role is development of individual potential. In that role, the manager is featured more as a counselor than as a judge, and the atmosphere is often different. Emphasis is on identifying potential and planning employees' growth opportunities and direction. Figure 7-3 shows the two potentially conflicting roles for performance appraisal.

Informal versus Systematic Appraisal

Performance appraisal can occur in two ways, informally or systematically. The *informal appraisal* is conducted whenever the supervisor feels it necessary. The

---

FIGURE 7-3 Conflicting Roles for Performance Appraisal?

ADMINISTRATIVE USES	**DEVELOPMENT USES**
• Compensation	• Identifying strengths
• Promotion	• Identifying areas for growth
• Dismissal	• Development planning
• Downsizing	• Coaching and career
• Layoffs	planning

PERFORMANCE APPRAISAL

---

day-to-day working relationship between a manager and an employee offers an opportunity for the employee's performance to be judged. This judgment is communicated through conversation on the job, over coffee, or by on-the-spot examination of a particular piece of work. Informal appraisal is especially appropriate when time is an issue. The longer feedback is delayed, the less likely it is to lead to behavior change. Frequent informal feedback to employees can also prevent surprises when the formal evaluation is communicated.

A *systematic appraisal* is used when the contact between manager and employee is formal, and a system is in place to report managerial impressions and observations on employee performance. Although informal appraisal is useful, it should not take the place of formal appraisal. Formal appraisals typically are conducted once or twice a year, most often annually, near the employee's anniversary date. For new employees, common timing is to conduct an appraisal ninety days after employment, again at six months, and annually thereafter. "Probationary" or new employees, or those who are new and in a trial period, should be evaluated frequently—perhaps weekly for the first month and monthly thereafter until the end of the introductory period for new employees. After that, annual reviews may be sufficient. Indeed, some argue that performance can be appraised too often.[2] A regular time interval is the feature of systematic appraisals that distinguishes them from informal appraisals. Both employees and managers are aware that performance will be reviewed on a regular basis, and they can plan for performance discussions. In addition, informal appraisals should be conducted whenever a manager feels they are desirable.

Who Conducts Appraisals?

Performance appraisal can be done by anyone familiar with the performance of individual employees. Possibilities include the following:

▶ Supervisors who rate their employees
▶ Employees who rate their superiors
▶ Team members who rate each other
▶ Employee self-appraisal
▶ Outside sources
▶ Multisource (360°) appraisal

The first method is the most common. The immediate superior has the sole responsibility for appraisal in most organizations, although it is common practice to have the appraisal reviewed and approved by the supervisor's boss. Any system should include a face-to-face discussion between rater and ratee.

Supervisor Rating of Subordinates. Traditional rating of employees by supervisors is based on the assumption that the immediate supervisor is the one person most qualified to evaluate the employee's performance realistically, objectively, and fairly. Toward this end, some supervisors keep performance logs noting what their employees have done. These logs provide specific examples to use when doing ratings.

Employee Rating of Managers. The concept of having supervisors and managers rated by employees or group members is being used in a number of organizations today. A prime example of this type of rating takes place in colleges and universities, where students evaluate the performance of professors in the classroom. Industry also uses employee ratings for management development purposes.

There are advantages to having employees rate managers. Employee ratings can be quite useful in identifying competent managers. This type of rating program can help make the manager more responsive to employees, and employee appraisals can be the basis for coaching as part of a career development effort for the managers. However, a major disadvantage of receiving employee ratings is the negative reaction many superiors have to being evaluated by employees.

Team/Peer Ratings. The use of peer groups as raters is another type of appraisal with potential both to help and to hurt. For example, if a group of sales representatives meets as a committee to talk about one another's ratings, then they may share ideas that could be used to improve the performance of lower-rated individuals. Alternatively, the criticisms could lead to future work relationships being affected negatively. Peer ratings are especially useful when supervisors do not have the opportunity to observe each employee's performance, but other work group members do.[3] Although team members may have good information on one another's performance, they may not choose to share it. They may unfairly attack or "go easy" to spare feelings. Some organizations attempt to overcome such problems by using anonymous appraisals and/or having a consultant or manager interpret peer ratings. However, using nonteam members to facilitate the rating process does not necessarily result in the system being seen as more fair by those being rated. Whatever the solution, team/peer performance ratings are important and probably inevitable, especially where work teams are used extensively.

Employee Self-Ratings. Self-appraisal can work in certain situations. It is best used as a self-development tool that forces employees to think about their strengths and weaknesses and set goals for improvement. If an employee is working in isolation or possesses unique talents, the employee may be the only one qualified to rate his or her own behavior.

Outside Raters. Rating also may be done by outsiders. Outside experts may be called in to review the work of a college president, for example. A panel of division managers might evaluate a person's potential for advancement in an organization. Outsiders may furnish managers with professional assistance in making appraisals, but there are obvious disadvantages. The outsider may not know all the important contingencies within the organization. In addition, outsider appraisals are time-consuming and expensive.

Multisource Rating. Multisource feedback recognizes that the manager is no longer the sole source of performance appraisal information. Instead, feedback from various colleagues and constituencies is obtained and given to the manager, thus allowing the manager to help shape the feedback from all sources. The manager remains a focal point both to receive the feedback initially and to engage in appropriate follow-up, even in a 360° system. Thus, the manager's perception of an employee's performance is still an important part of the process.

METHODS FOR APPRAISING PERFORMANCE

Performance can be appraised using a number of different methods. Various methods are categorized into four major groups. After describing each method in this section, the discussion considers combinations of methods that may make more effective appraisals in some situations.

Category Rating Methods

The simplest methods for appraising performance are category rating methods, which require a manager to mark an employee's level of performance on a specific form divided into categories of performance. The graphic rating scale and checklist are common category rating methods.

Graphic Rating Scale. The **graphic rating scale** allows the rater to mark an employee's performance on a continuum. Because of its simplicity, this method is the one most frequently used. Figure 7-4 shows a graphic rating scale form used by managers to rate employees. The rater checks the appropriate rating on the scale for each duty listed. More detail can be added in the space for comments following each factor rated.

FIGURE 7-4   Sample Performance Appraisal Form (simplified)

Date Sent   **4/19/00**   Return by   **5/01/00**
Name   **Jane Doe**   Job TItle   **Receiving Clerk**
Department   **Receiving**   Supervisor   **Fred Smith**
Full-time   **x**   Part-time _____   Date of Hire   **5/12/98**
Rating Period: From   **5/12/99**   To: **5/12/00**
Reason for appraisal (check one):   Regular Interval **x**   Introductory ___   Counseling only ___   Discharge ___

Utilizing the following definitions, rate the performance on as I, M, or E.
I - Performance is below job requirements and **improvement is needed.**
M - Performance meets job requirements and is **meeting standards.**
E - Performance **exceeds** job requirements a **majority** of the time and is **exceeding standards.**

SPECIFIC JOB RESPONSIBILITIES: List the principal activities from the job summary, rate the performance on each job duty by placing an "X" on the rating scale at the appropriate location, and make appropriate comments to explain the rating.

| I | M | E |

Job Duty #1: Inventory receiving and checking
Explanation: _____
_____

| I | M | E |

Job Duty #2: Accuracy of records kept
Explanation: _____
_____

| I | M | E |

Attendance: (including absences and tardies):   Number of absences ___   Number of tardies ___
Explanation: _____
_____

Overall Rating: Based on the total performance, place the letter **I, M,** or **E** in the box provided that best describes the employee's overall performance.
Explanation: _____
_____

Graphic rating scales in many forms are used widely because they are easy to develop; however, they encourage errors on the part of the raters, who may depend too heavily on the form itself to define performance. Both graphic rating scales and the checklist (which follows) tend to focus much emphasis on the rating instrument itself and its limitations. Insofar as they fit the person and job being rated, the scales work well. However, if the instrument is a poor fit, managers who must use them frequently complain about "the rating form."

Checklist. The checklist is composed of a list of statements or words. Raters check statements most representative of the characteristics and performance of employees. The following are typical checklist statements:

_____ Can be expected to finish work on time
_____ Seldom agrees to work overtime
_____ Is cooperative and helpful
_____ Accepts criticism
_____ Strives for self-improvement

The checklist can be modified so that varying weights are assigned to the statements or words. The results can then be quantified. Usually, the weights are not known by the rating supervisor because they are tabulated by someone else, such as a member of the HR unit.

Comparative Methods

Comparative methods require that managers directly compare the performance of their employees against one another. Various means are used to conduct the comparisons.

Ranking. The **ranking** method consists of listing all employees from highest to lowest in performance. The primary drawback of the ranking method is that the size of the differences among individuals is not well defined. Ranking also means that someone must be last. It is possible that the last-ranked individual in one group would be the top employee in a different group. Further, ranking becomes very unwieldy if the group to be ranked is very large.

Forced Distribution. **Forced distribution** is a technique for distributing ratings that can be generated with any of the other methods. However, it does require a comparison among people in the work group under consideration.

With the forced distribution method, the ratings of employees' performance are distributed along a bell-shaped curve. There are several drawbacks to the forced distribution method. One problem is that a supervisor may resist placing any individual in the lowest (or the highest) group. Further, with small groups, there may be no reason to assume that a bell-shaped distribution of performance really exists.

Narrative Methods

Managers and HR specialists often are required to provide written appraisal information. Documentation and description are the essence of these methods. These records describe an employee's actions rather than indicating an actual rating.

Behavioral/Objectives Methods

In an attempt to overcome some of the difficulties of the methods just described, several different behavioral approaches have been used. Behavioral approaches hold promise for some situations in overcoming some of the problems with other methods. Behavioral rating approaches describe examples of employee job behaviors. These examples are "anchored," or measured, against a scale of performance levels. What constitutes various levels of performance is clearly defined. Spelling out the behavior associated with each level of performance helps minimize some of the problems noted earlier for other approaches.

Several problems associated with the behavioral approaches must be considered. First, developing and maintaining behaviorally anchored rating scales (BARSs) requires extensive time and effort. In addition, several appraisal forms are needed to accommodate different types of jobs in an organization. In a hospital, nurses, dietitians, and admission clerks all have different jobs; separate BARS forms would need to be developed for each distinct job.

Management by Objectives (MBO). Management by objectives (MBO) specifies the performance goals that an individual hopes to attain within an appropriate length of time. The objectives that each manager sets are derived from the overall goals and objectives of the organization, although MBO should not be a disguised means for a superior to dictate the objectives of individual managers or employees. Although not limited to the appraisal of managers, MBO is most often used for this purpose. Names for MBO include *appraisal by results, target-coaching, work planning and review, performance objectives,* and *mutual goal setting.*

No management tool is perfect, and certainly MBO is not appropriate for all employees or all organizations. Jobs with little or no flexibility are not compatible with MBO. The MBO process seems to be most useful with managerial personnel and employees who have a fairly wide range of flexibility and control over their jobs.

Rater Errors

There are many possible sources of error in the performance appraisal process. One of the major sources is mistakes made by the rater. There is no simple way to completely eliminate these errors, but making raters aware of them through training is helpful.

Problems of Varying Standards. When appraising employees, a manager should avoid using different standards and expectations for employees performing similar jobs, which is certain to incur the anger of employees. Such problems are likely to exist when ambiguous criteria and subjective weightings by supervisors are used.

Even if an employee actually has been appraised on the same basis as others, his or her perception is relevant. If a student felt a professor had graded his exam more stringently than another student's exam, he might ask the professor for an explanation. The student's opinion might not be changed by the professor's claim that she had "graded fairly." So it is with performance appraisals in a work situation. If performance appraisal information is to be helpful, the rater must use the same standards and weights for every employee and be able to defend the appraisal.

Central Tendency, Leniency, and Strictness Errors. Appraisers who rate all employees within a narrow range (usually the middle or average) commit a **central tendency error**. Rating patterns also may exhibit leniency or strictness. The *leniency error* occurs when ratings of all employees are at the high end of the scale. The *strictness error* occurs when a manager uses only the lower part of the scale to rate employees. Recent research on leniency strongly suggests that when performance evaluation is done for administrative purposes (for example, pay or promotion), the ratings are on average one-third standard deviation higher than when they are done for development purposes.[4]

Rater Bias. **Rater bias** occurs when a rater's values or prejudices distort the rating. Rater bias may be unconscious or quite intentional. If a manager has a strong dislike of certain ethnic groups, this bias is likely to result in distorted appraisal information for some people. Age, religion, seniority, sex, appearance, or other arbitrary classifications may be reflected in appraisals if the appraisal process is not properly designed. Examination of ratings by higher-level managers may help correct this problem.

Halo Effect. The **halo effect** occurs when a manager rates an employee high or low on all items because of one characteristic. An appraisal that shows the same rating on all characteristics may be evidence of the halo effect. Clearly specifying the categories to be rated, rating all employees on one characteristic at a time, and training raters to recognize the problem are some ways of reducing the halo effect.

Appraisal Feedback

Once appraisals have been completed, it is important to communicate them so that employees have a clear understanding of how they stand in the eyes of their immediate superiors and the organization. It is common for organizations to require that managers discuss appraisals with employees. The appraisal feedback interview can be used to clear up misunderstandings on both sides. In this interview, the manager should emphasize counseling and development, not just tell the employee, "Here is how you rate and why." The appraisal interview presents both an opportunity and a danger. If the interview is handled poorly, the employee may feel resentment, and conflict may result, which could be reflected in future work.[5]

Employees usually approach an appraisal interview with some concern. They often feel that discussions about performance are very personal and important to their continued job success. At the same time, they want to know how their manager feels they have been doing.

PERFORMANCE APPRAISALS AND THE LAW

The elements of a performance appraisal system that can survive court tests can be determined from existing case law. Various cases have provided guidance. The elements of a legally defensible performance appraisal are as follows:

▶ Performance appraisal criteria based on job analysis
▶ Absence of disparate impact and evidence of validity
▶ Formal evaluation criteria that limit managerial discretion
▶ Formal rating instrument
▶ Personal knowledge of and contact with appraised individual
▶ Training of supervisors in conducting appraisals
▶ Review process that prevents one manager acting alone from controlling an employee's career
▶ Counseling to help poor performers improve

It is clear that the courts are interested in fair and nondiscriminatory performance appraisals. Employers must decide how to design their appraisal systems to satisfy the courts, enforcement agencies, and their employees.[6]

Effective Performance Management

Regardless of the approach used, an understanding of what performance management is supposed to do is critical. When performance appraisal is used to develop employees as resources, it usually works. When management uses performance appraisal as a punishment or when raters fail to understand its limitations, it fails. The key is not which form or which method is used, but whether managers and employees understand its purposes. In its simplest form, a performance appraisal is a manager's observation: "Here are your strengths and weaknesses, and here is a way to shore up the weak areas." It can lead to higher employee motivation and satisfaction if done right.

Most systems can be improved by training supervisors, because conducting performance appraisal is a big part of a performance management system. Training should focus on minimizing rater errors and providing a common frame of reference on how raters observe and recall information.

NOTES

1. Fred Kniggendorf, "Helping Supervisors Define Standards of Performance," *HR Focus,* February 1998, 13.
2. Devaun M. Kite et al., "Can Managers Appraise Performance Too Often?," *Journal of Applied Business Research* 13, n.d., 41–51.
3. Carol Patton, "Panel of Peers," *Human Resource Executive,* June 5, 1998, 84–86.
4. I. M. Jawahar and Charles R. Williams, "Where All the Children Are Above Average," *Personnel Psychology* 50, 1997, 905–926.
5. Dick Gnote, "Painless Performance Appraisals Focus on Results, Behaviors," *HR Magazine,* October 1998, 52–58.
6. "Minimize Performance Evaluation Legal Risks," *Journal of Accountancy,* February 1998, 10.

SUGGESTED READINGS

Danny Langdon, *Aligning Performance,* Jossey-Bass, 1999.

Roy Lecky-Thompson, *Constructive Appraisals,* AMACOM, 1999.

James Smither, *Performance Appraisal: State of Art in Practice,* Jossey-Bass, 1998.

Brandon Toropov, *Manager's Portfolio of Model Performance Evaluations,* Prentice-Hall, 1999.

Bruce Tulgan, *FAST Feedback,* HRD Press, 1999.

SUGGESTED INTERNET RESOURCES

Competency Suite. Describes performance management and appraisal process tools and approaches.
http://www.competencysuite.com

Fred Pryor Seminars. Discusses appraisal tools and approaches to make performance appraisals more useful.
http://www.careertrack.com

CHAPTER 8

Compensation

Compensation is important both in attracting and retaining employees. An effective compensation system considers both internal fairness and external competitiveness.

Compensation systems in organizations must be linked to organizational objectives and strategies. But compensation also requires balancing the interests and costs of the employer with the expectations of employees. A compensation program in an organization has four objectives:

▸ Legal compliance with all appropriate laws and regulations
▸ Cost effectiveness for the organization
▸ Internal, external, and individual equity for employees
▸ Performance enhancement for the organization

THE NATURE OF COMPENSATION

Compensation is an important factor that affects why people choose to work at one organization over others. Employers must be reasonably competitive with several types of compensation in order to hire, keep, and reward performance of individuals in the organization.

Tangible components of a compensation program are of two general types (Figure 8-1). With the direct type of compensation, monetary rewards are provided by the employer. *Base pay* and *variable pay* are the most common forms of direct compensation. Indirect compensation commonly consists of employee *benefits*.

FIGURE 8-1 **Compensation Components**

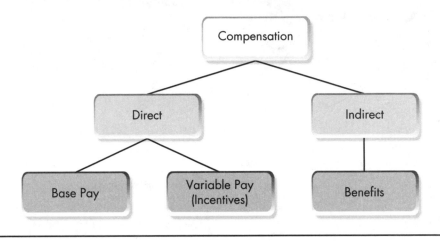

Base Pay

The basic compensation that an employee receives, usually as a wage or salary, is called **base pay**. Many organizations use two base pay categories, *hourly* and *salaried*, according to the way pay is distributed and the nature of the jobs. Hourly pay is the most common means of payment based on time; employees who are paid hourly are said to receive **wages**, which are payments directly calculated on the amount of time worked. In contrast, people who are paid salaries receive payments that are consistent from period to period despite the number of hours worked. Being salaried typically carries higher status for employees than being paid wages.

Variable Pay

Another type of direct pay is **variable pay**, which is compensation linked directly to performance accomplishments. The most common types of variable pay for most employees are bonuses and incentive program payments. For executives, it is common to have longer-term rewards such as stock options. Variable pay, including executive compensation, is discussed in more detail later.

Benefits

Many organizations provide numerous extrinsic rewards in an indirect manner. With indirect compensation, employees receive the tangible value of the rewards without receiving the actual cash. A **benefit** is an indirect reward, such as health insurance, vacation pay, or retirement pensions, given to an employee or group of employees as a part of organizational membership.

STRATEGIC COMPENSATION

Compensation decisions must be viewed strategically. Because so many organizational funds are spent on compensation-related activities, it is critical for top management and HR executives to view the "strategic" fit of compensation with the strategies and objectives of the organization. There are two basic compensation philosophies, which should be seen as opposite ends of a continuum. At one end of the continuum is the entitlement philosophy; at the other end, the performance-oriented philosophy. The **entitlement philosophy** can be seen in many organizations that traditionally have given automatic increases to their employees every year. Further, most of those employees receive the same or nearly the same percentage increase each year. Employees and managers who subscribe to the entitlement philosophy believe that individuals who have worked another year are *entitled* to a raise in base pay, and that all incentives and benefit programs should continue and be increased, regardless of changing industry or economic conditions. Where a **performance philosophy** is followed, no one is guaranteed increased compensation just for adding another year to organizational service. Instead, pay and incentives are based on performance differences among employees. Employees who perform well get larger compensation increases; those who do not perform satisfactorily receive little or no increase in compensation. Thus, employees who perform satisfactorily should keep up or advance in relation to a broad view of the labor market for their jobs, whereas poor or marginal performers should fall behind.

Cost-Effectiveness and Labor Market Positioning

Another strategic design consideration for compensation systems is to balance the costs of attracting and retaining employees with the competitive pressures in the industry. Considering these pressures is particularly important when the organization faces a very tight labor market for workers with specific skills. Most compensation programs are designed to reward employees for the tasks, duties, and responsibilities performed. It is the jobs done that determine, to a large extent, which employees have higher base rates than others. Employees are paid more for doing jobs that require more variety of tasks, more knowledge and skills, greater physical effort, or more demanding working conditions.

Competency-Based Pay

A growing number of organizations are paying employees for the competencies they have rather than just for the specific tasks they perform. Paying for competencies rewards employees who are more versatile and have continued to develop their competencies. In *knowledge-based pay* (KBP) or *skill-based pay* (SBP) systems, employees start at a base level of pay and receive increases as they learn to do other jobs or gain other skills and therefore become more valuable to the employer.

Broadbanding

Using an approach closely related to competency-based compensation, many organizations have revised their hierarchical pay structures. **Broadbanding**, which uses fewer pay grades having broader ranges than traditional compensation systems, is increasingly being used.[1]

Use of Variable Pay

Another growing compensation approach is the use of variable pay throughout the organization. Traditionally in many organizations, most employees receive compensation based either on wages or salaries. Except for executives, few individuals receive additional pay tied to performance other than annual raises in their base pay amounts.

Currently, variable pay programs have been extensively adopted throughout many organizations and for all levels of employees. Widespread use of various incentive plans, team bonuses, organizational gainsharing programs, and other designs have been implemented in order to link growth in compensation to results.

Team-Based Compensation

Another compensation design issue that has grown in importance is team-based compensation. As organizations have shifted to using work teams, a logical concern is how to develop compensation programs that build on the team concept. It becomes even trickier because organizations are compensating individuals who work in teams. Paying everyone on teams the same amount even though there are differing competencies and levels of performance obviously may create equity concerns for individual employees. Many organizations use team rewards as variable pay above base pay. For base pay, individuals are compensated using competency- or skill-based approaches.

Behavioral Aspects of Compensation

Behavioral factors affect all types of compensation. Most people in work organizations are there in order to gain rewards for their efforts. Except in volunteer organizations, people expect to receive fair value in the form of compensation. Whether regarding base pay, variable pay, or benefits, the extent to which employees perceive they are receiving fair value often affects their performance and how they view their jobs and employers. This is the concept of **equity**, which is the perceived fairness of the relation between what a person does (inputs) and what the person receives (outcomes). Internally, equity means that employees receive compensation in relation to the KSAs they use in their jobs, as well as their responsibilities and accomplishments.

Two key issues that relate to internal equity are *procedural justice* and *distributive justice*. **Procedural justice** is the perceived fairness of the process and procedures used to make decisions about employees, including their pay.[2] As it applies to compensation, the process of determining the base pay for jobs, the allocation of pay increases, and the measurement of performance must be perceived as fair. Two critical issues are: (1) How appropriate and fair is the process used to assign jobs to pay grades? and (2) How are the pay ranges for those jobs established?

Another related issue that must be considered is **distributive justice**, which refers to the perceived fairness of the amounts given for performance. This aspect of equity refers to how pay relates to performance. For instance, if a hardworking employee whose performance is outstanding receives the same across-the-board raise as an employee with attendance problems and mediocre performance, then greater inequity may be perceived.

It is important for HR professionals and managers to develop, administer, and maintain compensation plans that are perceived equitably by employees. The consequence of an equitable compensation program is that individuals are more likely to be attracted to and take jobs in organizations where employees do not voice widespread concerns about equity.

LEGAL CONSTRAINTS ON PAY SYSTEMS

Compensation systems must comply with a myriad of government constraints. Minimum-wage standards and hours of work are two important areas addressed by the laws.

Fair Labor Standards Act (FLSA)

The major law affecting compensation is the Fair Labor Standards Act (FLSA). The act has three major objectives:

▶ Establish a minimum wage floor.
▶ Discourage inappropriate use of child labor.
▶ Encourage limits on the number of weekly hours employees work through overtime provisions (exempt and nonexempt status).

Minimum Wage. The FLSA sets a minimum wage to be paid to the broad spectrum of covered employees. The actual minimum wage can be changed only by congressional action. A lower minimum-wage level is set for "tipped" employees who work in such firms as restaurants, but their payment must at least equal the minimum wage when *average* tips are included.

Child Labor. The child labor provisions of the FLSA set the minimum age for employment with unlimited hours at age 16. For hazardous occupations, the minimum age is 18. Those 14 to 15 years old may work outside school hours with certain limitations.

Exempt and Nonexempt Status. Under the FLSA, employees are classified as exempt or nonexempt. **Exempt** employees are those who hold positions classified as executive, administrative, professional, or outside sales, to whom employers are not required to pay overtime. **Nonexempt** employees are those who must be paid overtime under the Fair Labor Standards Act.

Three major factors are considered in determining whether an individual holds an exempt position:

▶ Discretionary authority for independent action
▶ Percentage of time spent performing routine, manual, or clerical work
▶ Earnings level

Figure 8-2 shows the impact of these factors on each type of exemption. It is useful to note that the earnings levels are basically meaningless, because they have not changed in years despite increases in the minimum wage. These inconsistencies are due to political disagreements among employers, unions, legislators, and federal regulators.

Overtime. The FLSA establishes overtime pay requirements. Its provisions set overtime pay at one and one-half times the regular pay rate for all hours in excess of 40 per week, except for employees who are not covered by the FLSA. Overtime provisions do not apply to farm workers, who have a lower minimum-wage schedule.

Compensatory Time Off. Often called *comp time,* **compensatory time off** is given in lieu of payment for extra time worked. However, unless it is given at the rate of one and one-half times the hours worked over a 40-hour week, comp time is illegal in the private sector. Also, comp time cannot be carried over from one pay period to another. The only major exception to those provisions is for public-sector employees, such as fire and police employees, and a limited number of other workers.

Independent Contractor Regulations

The growing use of contingent workers by many organizations has called attention to another group of legal regulations—those identifying the criteria that independent contractors must meet.[3] The criteria for deciding independent contractor status have been identified by the Internal Revenue Service (IRS), and most other federal and state entities rely on those criteria.

Equal Pay and Pay Equity

Various legislative efforts have addressed the issue of wage discrimination on the basis of gender. The Equal Pay Act was passed as a major amendment to the FLSA in 1963. The original act and subsequent amendments focus on wage discrimination on the basis of sex. The act applies to both men and women and prohibits paying different wage scales to men and women performing substan-

FIGURE 8-2   Wage/Hour Status Under Fair Labor Standards Act

EXEMPTION CATEGORY	A DISCRETIONARY AUTHORITY	B PERCENTAGE OF TIME	C EARNINGS LEVELS
Executive	1. Primary duty is managing 2. Regularly directs work of at least two others 3. Authority to hire/fire or recommend these	1. Must spend 20% or less time doing clerical, manual, routine work (less than 40% in retail or service establishments)	1. Paid salary at $155/wk or $250/wk if meets A1–A2
Administrative	1. Primarily responsible for nonmanual or office work related to management policies 2. Regularly exercises discretion and independent judgment and makes important decisions 3. Regularly assists executives and works under general supervision	1. Must spend 20% or less time doing clerical, manual, routine work (less than 40% in retail or service establishments)	1. Paid salary at $155/wk or $250/wk if meets A1–A2
Professional	1. Performs work requiring knowledge of an advanced field *or* creative and original artistic work *or* works as teacher in educational system 2. Must do work that is predominantly intellectual and varied	1. Must spend 20% or less time doing nonprofessional work	1. Paid salary at least $170/wk or $250/wk if meets A1
Outside Sales	1. Customarily works away from employer site *and* 2. Sells tangible or intangible items *or* 3. Obtains orders or contracts for services	1. Must spend 20% or less time doing work other than outside selling	1. No salary test

Note: For more details, see *Executive, Administrative, Professional, and Outside Sales Exemptions under the Fair Labor Standards Act,* WH Publication no. 1363 (Washington, DC: U.S. Department of Labor, Employment Standards Administration, Wage and Hour Division).

tially the same jobs. Pay differences are justifiable on the basis of merit (better performance), seniority (longer service), quantity or quality of work, or almost any factor other than gender. Similar pay must be given for jobs requiring equal skills, equal effort, or equal responsibility or jobs done under similar working conditions.

Pay equity is a different issue from that of equal pay for equal work. *Pay equity* is the concept that the pay for all jobs requiring comparable knowledge, skills, and abilities should be similar even if actual duties and market rates differ significantly. Except where state laws (in the United States) or provincial laws (in Canada) have required pay equity, simply showing that there are pay differences for jobs that are different has not been sufficient to prove discrimination in court.

WAGE AND SALARY ADMINISTRATION

The development, implementation, and ongoing maintenance of a base pay system usually is described as **wage and salary administration**. The purpose of wage and salary administration is to provide pay that is both competitive and equitable. Underlying the administered activities are pay policies that set the overall direction of pay within the organization.

Pay Policies

Organizations must develop formal pay policies as general guidelines to provide for coordination, consistency, and fairness in compensating employees. These pay policies are an outgrowth of the answers to the compensation philosophy issues discussed earlier. For example, following a pay-for-performance philosophy requires incorporating performance appraisal results into the pay adjustment process. However, a more entitlement-oriented philosophy will require developing policies in automatic step increases based on length of service for hourly employees.

Market Positioning. A major policy decision must be made about the comparative level of pay the organization wants to maintain. Specifically, an employer must identify how competitive it wishes to be in the external market for employees. Organizations usually want to "pay market"—that is, to match the "going rates" paid to employees by competitive organizations in order to ensure external equity.

Some organizations choose to *lead* the market by paying above-market rates. This policy aids in attracting and retaining employees. In contrast, some employers may deliberately choose to *lag* the market by paying below market. If there is an excess of qualified workers in an area, an adequate number of people may be willing to work for lower pay.

Market Pricing. Some employers do not establish a formal wage and salary system. Smaller employers particularly may assume that the pay set by other employers is an accurate reflection of a job's worth, so they set their pay rates at **market price**, the typical wage paid for a job in the immediate labor market.

FIGURE 8-3 **Compensation Administration Process**

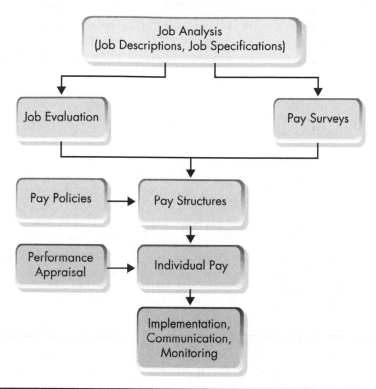

Unions and Compensation

A major variable affecting an employer's pay policies is whether any employees are represented by a labor union. In nonunion organizations, employers have significantly more flexibility in determining pay levels and policies. Unionized employees usually have their pay set according to the terms of a collective bargaining contract between their employer and the union that represents them. Because pay is a visible issue, it is natural for unions to emphasize pay levels.

DEVELOPING A BASE PAY SYSTEM

As Figure 8-3 shows, the development of a wage and salary system assumes that accurate job descriptions and job specifications are available. The job descriptions then are used in two activities: *job evaluation* and *pay surveys*. These activities are designed to ensure that the pay system is both internally equitable and externally competitive. The data compiled in these two activities are used to design *pay structures,* including *pay grades* and minimum-to-maximum *pay ranges*.

Job Evaluation

Job evaluation provides a systematic basis for determining the relative worth of jobs within an organization. It flows from the job analysis process and is based on job descriptions and job specifications. In a job evaluation, every job in an organization is examined and ultimately evaluated according to the following features:

- ▶ Relative importance of the job
- ▶ KSAs needed to perform the job
- ▶ Difficulty of the job

It is important that employees perceive their pay as appropriate in relation to pay for jobs performed by others. Because jobs may vary widely in an organization, it is particularly important to identify **benchmark jobs**—jobs that are found in many other organizations and are performed by several individuals who have similar duties that are relatively stable and that require similar KSAs.

Several methods are used to determine internal job worth through job evaluation. All methods have the same general objective, but they differ in complexity and means of measurement. Regardless of the method used, the intent is to develop a usable, measurable, and realistic system to determine compensation in an organization.

Ranking Method. The ranking method is one of the simplest methods of job evaluation. It places jobs in order, ranging from highest to lowest in value to the organization. The entire job is considered rather than the individual components.[4] Several different methods of ranking are available, but all present problems.

Classification Method. In the classification method of job evaluation, descriptions of each class of jobs are written. Then each job in the organization is put into a classification grade according to the class description it matches the best.

Point Method. The point method, the most widely used job evaluation method, is more sophisticated than the ranking and classification methods. It breaks down jobs into various compensable factors and places weights, or *points,* on them. A **compensable factor** is one used to identify a job value that is commonly present throughout a group of jobs. The factors are determined from the job analysis. For example, for jobs in warehouse and manufacturing settings, *physical demands, hazards encountered,* and *working environment* may be identified as factors and weighted heavily. However, in most office and clerical jobs, those factors are of little importance.

A special type of point method used by a consulting firm, the Hay Group, has received widespread application, although it is most often used with exempt employees. The Hay system uses three factors and numerically measures the degree to which each of these factors is required in each job. The three factors and their subfactors are as follows:[5]

Know-How	Problem Solving	Accountability
▶ Functional expertise	▶ Environment	▶ Freedom to act
▶ Managerial skills	▶ Challenge	▶ Impact of end results
▶ Human relations		▶ Magnitude

The point method has grown in popularity for several reasons. It is a relatively straight-forward system to use because it considers the components of a job rather than the total job and is much more comprehensive than either the ranking or classification method. Once points have been determined and a job evaluation point manual has been developed, the method can be used easily by people who are not specialists. The system can be understood by managers and employees, which gives it a definite advantage.

Factor Comparison Method. The factor comparison method is a quantitative and complex combination of the ranking and point methods. Factor comparison not only tells which jobs are worth more but also indicates how much more, so that factor values can be more easily converted to monetary wages.

Integrated and Computerized Job Evaluation. Increasingly, organizations are linking the components of wage and salary programs through computerized and statistical techniques. Using a bank of compensable factors, employers can select those factors that are most relevant for the different job families in the organization.

Gender Issues and Job Evaluation. Critics have charged that traditional job evaluation programs place less weight on knowledge, skills, and working conditions for many female-dominated jobs in office and clerical areas than on the same factors for male-dominated jobs in craft and manufacturing areas. Also, jobs typically are compared only with others in the same job "family." As discussed earlier, advocates of pay equity view the disparity between men's jobs and women's jobs as evidence of gender discrimination. These advocates also have attacked typical job evaluations as being gender-biased.

Pay Surveys

Another part of building a pay system is surveying the pay that other organizations provide for similar jobs. A pay survey is a collection of data on compensation rates for workers performing similar jobs in other organizations. An employer may use surveys conducted by other organizations, or it may decide to conduct its own survey. Many different surveys are available from a variety of sources. Whether available electronically or in printed form, national surveys on many jobs and industries come from the U.S. Department of Labor, Bureau of Labor Statistics, and through national trade associations.

FIGURE 8-4 Establishing Pay Structures

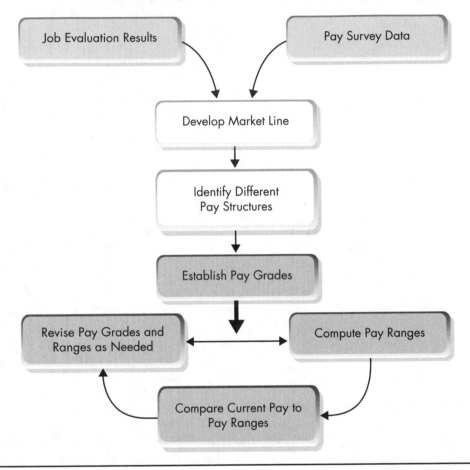

Pay Structures

Once survey data has been gathered, pay structures can be developed by the process depicted in Figure 8-4. Job evaluation results and pay survey data are compared through the use of the *least-squares regression* method. Also, a curvilinear relationship can be shown by use of multiple regression and other statistical techniques. The end result is the development of a **market line**. This line shows the relationship between job value, as determined by job evaluation points, and pay survey rates.

In organizations there are a number of different job families. The pay survey data may reveal that there are different levels of pay due to market factors, which may lead to firms establishing several different pay structures, rather than just one structure. Examples of some common pay structures are: (1) hourly and salaried; (2) office, plant, technical, professional, and managerial; and (3) clerical, information technology, professional, supervisory, management, and executive.

Establishing Pay Grades. In the process of establishing a pay structure, organizations use **pay grades** to group individual jobs having approximately the same job worth. While there are no set rules to be used in establishing pay grades, some overall suggestions have been made. Generally, from eleven to seventeen grades are used in small companies. However, as discussed earlier, a number of employers are reducing the number of grades by *broadbanding*.

Pay Ranges. The pay range for each pay grade also must be established. Using the market line as a starting point, the employer can determine maximum and minimum pay levels for each pay grade by making the market line the midpoint line of the new pay structure. (See Figure 8-5.) For example, in a particular pay grade the maximum value may be 20% above the midpoint and the minimum value 20% below it.

Individual Pay Issues

Once managers have determined pay ranges, they can set the specific pay for individuals. Each dot on the graph in Figure 8-5 represents an individual employee's current pay in relation to the pay ranges that have been developed. Setting a range for each pay grade gives flexibility by allowing individuals to progress within a grade instead of having to be moved to a new grade each time they receive a raise. Regardless of how well constructed a pay structure is, there usually are a few individuals whose pay is lower than the minimum or higher than the maximum. A **red-circled employee** is an incumbent who is paid above the range set for the job. An individual whose pay is below the range is a **green-circled employee**.

Pay Compression. One major problem many employers face is **pay compression**, which occurs when the range of pay differences among individuals with different levels of experience and performance becomes small. Pay compression occurs for a number of reasons, but the major one involves the situation in which labor market pay levels increase more rapidly than an employee's pay adjustments. Such situations have become prevalent in many occupational areas, particularly those in the information technology field.[6]

Pay Increases. Once pay ranges have been developed and individuals' placements within the ranges identified, managers must look at adjustment to individual pay. There are several ways to determine pay increases. Many employers profess to have a pay system based on performance. Consequently, some system for integrating appraisals and pay changes must be developed and applied equally. Often, this integration is done through the use of a *pay adjustment matrix* or *salary guide chart*. Pay adjustment matrices base adjustments in part on a per-

FIGURE 8-5 Example of Pay Grades and Pay Ranges

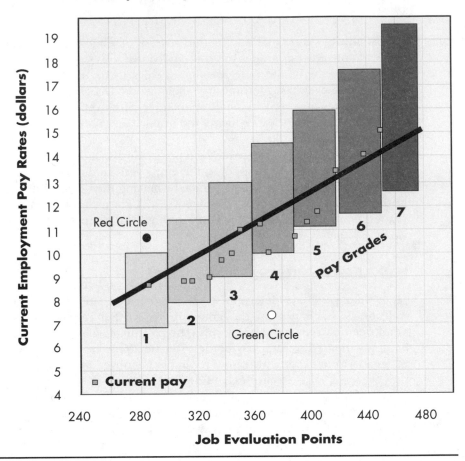

son's **compa-ratio**, which is the pay level divided by the midpoint of the pay range. **Seniority**, or time spent in the organization or on a particular job, can be used as the basis for pay increases. Pay adjustments based on seniority often are set as automatic steps once a person has been employed the required length of time.

Cost-of-Living Adjustments (COLA). A common pay-raise practice is the use of a standard raise or *cost-of-living adjustment* (COLA). Giving all employees a standard percentage increase enables them to maintain the same real wages in a period of economic inflation. Often, these adjustments are tied to changes in the Consumer Price Index (CPI) or some other general economic measure. However, numerous studies have revealed that the CPI overstates the actual cost of living.

FIGURE 8-6   Executive Compensation Components

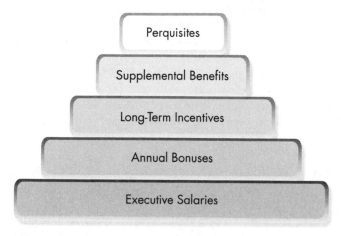

Most employees who receive pay increases, either for merit or seniority, first have their base pay adjusted and then receive an increase in the amount of their regular monthly or weekly paycheck. In contrast, a **lump-sum increase (LSI)** is a one-time payment of all or part of a yearly pay increase. The pure LSI approach does not increase the base pay. Some organizations place a limit on how much of a merit increase can be taken as a lump-sum payment. Other organizations split the lump sum into two checks, each representing one-half of the year's pay raise.

EXECUTIVE COMPENSATION

Many organizations, especially large ones, administer executive compensation somewhat differently than compensation for lower-level employees. An executive typically is someone in the top two levels of an organization, such as Chief Executive Officer (CEO), President, or Senior Vice-President. As Figure 8-6 shows, the common components of executive compensation are *salaries, annual bonuses, long-term incentives, supplemental benefits,* and *perquisites.*

Two objectives influence executive compensation: (1) ensuring that the total compensation packages for executives are competitive with the compensation packages in other firms that might employ them, and (2) tying the overall performance of the organization over a period of time to the compensation that is paid to executives. It is the second objective that critics of executive compensation believe is not being met. In many organizations, it appears that the levels of executive compensation may be unreasonable and not linked closely to organizational performance.

Performance-based incentives attempt to tie executive compensation to the long-term growth and success of the organization. However, whether the emphasis is really on the long term or merely represents a series of short-term rewards is controversial. Short-term rewards based on quarterly or annual performance may not result in the kind of long-run-oriented decisions necessary for the company to continue to do well.

A **stock option** gives an individual the right to buy stock in a company, usually at an advantageous price. Different types of stock options have been used, depending on the tax laws in effect. Stock options have increased in use as a component of executive compensation during the past ten years, and employers may use a variety of very specialized and technical approaches to them, which are beyond the scope of this discussion. However, the overall trend is toward using stock options as performance-based long-term incentives.

Executive benefits may include some items that other employees do not receive. For example, executive health plans with no co-payments and with no limitations on deductibles or physician choice are popular among small and medium-sized businesses. Corporate-owned life insurance on the life of the executive is popular and pays *both* the executive's estate and the company in the event of death. Trusts of various kinds may be designed by the company to help the executive deal with estate issues. Deferred compensation is another possible means used to help executives with tax liabilities caused by incentive compensation plans.

In addition to the regular benefits received by all employees, executives often receive benefits called perquisites. **Perquisites (perks)** are special executive benefits—usually noncash items such as private club memberships or first class air travel privileges. Perks are useful in tying executives to organizations and in demonstrating their importance to the companies.

The Role of the Board of Directors in Executive Compensation

In most organizations the board of directors is the major policy-setting entity. The **compensation committee** is usually a subgroup of the board of directors composed of directors who are not officers of the firm. Compensation committees generally make recommendations to the board of directors on overall pay policies, salaries for top officers, supplemental compensation such as stock options and bonuses, and additional perks for executives. But the "independence" of board compensation committees increasingly has been criticized. The link between the independence of board compensation committees and organization performances is crucial. If the compensation committee's decisions about executive variable pay lead to higher organizational performance, then the composition of the compensation committee is less of an issue.

Criticism of Executive Compensation

The biggest criticism of executive compensation levels is that even though the elements of executive compensation are supposed to be linked to organizational performance, in many companies the reality is that many executives get large compensation packages and produce mediocre to poor organizational results. Critics point to numerous examples of CEOs and other senior managers getting large rewards even when organizational performance declines.

"Golden Parachutes" for Executives

A special perk available to some executives, a **golden parachute**, provides protection and security to executives in the event that they lose their jobs or their firms are acquired by other firms. Typically, employment contracts are written to give special compensation to executives if they are negatively affected in an acquisition or merger. Golden parachutes often are criticized for giving executives protection, while lower- and middle-level managers and other employees are left vulnerable when mergers or acquisitions occur.

Undoubtedly, the criticisms of executive compensation will continue as huge payouts occur, particularly if organizational performance has been weak. Hopefully, boards of directors of more corporations will address the need to better link organizational performance with variable pay rewards for executives and other employees.

NOTES

1. Kenan S. Abosch and Beverly L. Hmurovic, "A Traveler's Guide to Broadbanding," *ACA Journal*, Summer 1998, 38–47.
2. Anthony T. Cobb, Mike Vest, and Fred Hills, "Who Delivers Justice?: Source Perceptions of Procedural Fairness," *Journal of Applied Social Psychology* 27, 1997, 1021–1040.
3. Michael N. Wolfe, "Classification of Workers: Independent Contractor vs. Employee," *ACA Journal*, Summer 1998, 6–15.
4. Institute for Adminstration and Management (IOMA)
   Contains information on pay surveys available and pay studies done on various industries and job families.
   http://www.ioma.com
5. For a detailed discussion of the Hay system, see Richard I. Henderson, *Compensation Management in a Knowledge-Based World*, 7th ed. (Englewood Cliffs, NJ: Prentice-Hall, 1997), 277–294.
6. Marilyn Moats Kennedy, "Are You a Victim of 'Salary Compression'?," *Manager's Intelligence Report*, 1998, 1.

SUGGESTED READINGS

Dorothy R. Berger and Lance A. Berger, *The Compensation Handbook*, McGraw-Hill, 1999.

Thomas J. Bergman, Vida Scarpello, and Frederick S. Hills, *Compensation Decision Making*, 3rd ed., Harcourt, 1999.

Glenn Parker, Jerry McAdams, and David Zielinski, *Rewarding Teams*, Jossey-Bass, 2000.

Howard Risher, *Aligning Pay and Results*, AMACOM, 1999.

SUGGESTED INTERNET RESOURCES

Economic Research Institute. Provides compensation and pay survey information.
http://www.erieri.com

World at Work. Contains extensive compensation information and resources from this association, formerly the American Compensation Association.
http://www.worldatwork.org

CHAPTER 9

Variable Pay and Benefits

Additional compensation may be based on individual, team, and organizational performance through variable pay programs. Employee benefits are a significant cost to organizations, but they are highly desired by employees.

VARIABLE PAY: INCENTIVES FOR PERFORMANCE

Employers increasingly are recognizing that the definition of compensation must be extended beyond base pay to include variable pay and employee benefits. **Variable pay** is compensation linked to individual, team, and/or organization performance. Also known as *incentives,* variable pay plans are attempts to tie tangible rewards to performance beyond normal expectations. The philosophical foundation of variable pay rests on several basic assumptions:

▶ Some jobs contribute more to organizational success than others.
▶ Some people perform better than others.
▶ Employees who perform better should receive more compensation.
▶ A portion of some employees' total compensation should be given to reward performance above expectations.

Employee benefits are available in a smorgasbord of indirect compensation, such as pensions, health insurance, time off with pay, and other forms. This chapter examines both of these types of additional compensation.

Variable pay plans can be established that focus on individual performance, team or group performance, and organization-wide performance. An important feature of variable pay plans is that incentives may increase the degree of cooperation in teams, whereas individual incentives do not.

FIGURE 9-1 Types of Variable Pay Plans

Individual	Group (Team)	Organization
		• Profit sharing
• Piece rate	• Gainsharing rewards	
• Sales commissions		• Employee stock options
• Bonuses	• Quality improvement rewards	
• Special recognitions (trips, merchandise)		• Executive stock options
• Safety awards	• Labor cost reduction payouts	
• Attendance bonuses		• Deferred compensation

Individual incentives are given to reward the effort and performance of individuals. Some of the most common means of providing individuals variable pay are piece-rate systems, sales commissions, and bonuses.

When an entire work group is rewarded for its performance, more cooperation among the members is required and usually forthcoming. The most common types of **team or group incentives** are *gainsharing plans,* in which employee teams or groups that meet certain goals share in the gains measured against performance targets. **Organization incentives** reward people for the performance of the entire organization. This approach may reduce individual and team competition, and assumes that all employees working together can generate better organizational results that lead to better financial performance. These programs share some of the financial gains to the firm through payments to employees, which often are paid as an additional percentage of each employee's base pay. Also, organizational incentives may be given as a lump-sum amount to employees, or different amounts may be given to different levels of employees throughout the organization. Figure 9-1 shows some of the programs under each type.

As variable pay has grown in popularity, it has become evident that these plans have both succeeded and failed. The reactions of employees are crucial to how variable pay plans are accepted. It is interesting that in a study of over two-thousand workers from a variety of companies, most respondents said they want performance rewards included in their base pay, rather than as one-time payments. Also, the employees strongly preferred individual rewards over team or organization incentives.[1] This study and others highlight the fact that neither of the polar extremes—the view that incentives do not work or the view that incentives are a panacea—appears to be the case. Also, the enthusiasm that many employers and managers have for variable pay plans is not matched by many workers. The key to success seems to be to combine incentives with employee participation in the process. In summary, it appears that variable pay plans can be successful under certain circumstances.

Guidelines for Variable Pay Plans

Providing variable pay through incentive systems can be complex and can take many forms. However, certain general guidelines are useful in establishing and maintaining successful variable pay systems:

▶ Recognize organizational culture and resources.
▶ Make variable pay plans understandable.
▶ Keep incentive plans current.
▶ Tie variable pay to desired performance.
▶ Recognize individual differences.
▶ Identify variable pay separate from base pay.

INDIVIDUAL INCENTIVES

Individual incentive systems attempt to relate individual effort to pay. The most basic individual incentive system is the **piece-rate system,** whether of the straight or differential type. Despite their incentive value, piece-rate systems are difficult to use because standards for many types of jobs are difficult and costly to determine. In some instances, the costs of determining and maintaining the standards may be greater than the benefits derived. Jobs in which individuals have limited control over output or in which high standards of quality are necessary also may be unsuited to piecework.

Bonuses

Individual employees may receive additional compensation payments in the form of a **bonus,** which is a one-time payment that does not become part of the employee's base pay. Generally, bonuses are less costly to the employer than other pay increases because they do not become part of employees' base wages, upon which future percentage increases are figured. Growing in popularity, bonuses often are used at the executive levels of an organization, but also are spreading to lower-level jobs.

Special Individual Incentive Programs

Numerous special incentive programs provide awards to individuals. These programs can take different forms, ranging from one-time contests for meeting performance targets to rewards for performance over time, such as safe-driving awards given for truck drivers who have no accidents or violations during a year. Although special programs also can be developed for groups and for entire organizations, these programs often focus on rewarding only high-performing individuals.

Sales Compensation and Incentives

Compensation paid to some sales and marketing employees is partly or entirely tied to sales performance. Better-performing salespeople receive more total compensation than those selling less. Successfully using variable sales compensation requires establishing clear performance criteria and measures. Generally, no more than three sales performance measures should be used in a sales compensation plan.[2]

Sales compensation plans are generally of several different types. The types are based on the degree to which total compensation includes some variable pay tied to sales performance. A survey of over 260 firms found that plans providing salary with bonus (37%) and salary with commission and bonus (35%) were the most-used types. Less used were plans providing commission only (24%) and salary only (5%).[3]

Some firms pay salespeople only a salary. The salary-only approach is useful when serving and retaining existing accounts is being emphasized more than generating new sales and accounts.

Straight Commission. An individual incentive system widely used in sales jobs is the **commission**, which is compensation computed as a percentage of sales in units or dollars. Commissions are integrated into the pay given to sales workers in three common ways: straight commission, salary plus commission, and bonuses.

Salary Plus Commission or Bonuses. The most frequently used form of sales compensation is the salary plus commission, which combines the stability of a salary with the performance aspect of a commission. Many organizations pay salespeople salaries and then offer bonuses as a percentage of base pay tied to meeting various levels of sales targets or other criteria. A common split is 70% salary to 30% commission, although the split varies by industry and with other factors.

TEAM-BASED INCENTIVES

The growing use of work teams in organizations has implications for compensation of the teams and their members. Interestingly, while the use of teams has increased significantly in the past few years, the question of how to equitably compensate the individuals who compose the team remains one of the biggest challenges. As Figure 9-2 notes, there are several reasons why organizations have established group or team variable pay plans, and evidently these goals are being met in a number of organizations.

FIGURE 9-2   Why Organizations Establish Team Variable Pay Plans

TEAM VARIABLE PAY

- Enhances Productivity
- Ties Earnings to Team Performance
- Improves Quality
- Aids Recruiting and Retention of Employees
- Improves Employee Morale

Types of Team Incentives

Team-based reward systems use various ways of compensating individuals. The components often include individual wages and salaries in addition to team-based rewards. Most team-based organizations continue to pay individuals based either on the jobs performed or the individuals' competencies and capabilities. Several decisions about methods of distributing and allocating team rewards must be made.

Distributing Team Incentives

The two primary approaches for distributing team rewards are as follows:

▶ *Same-size reward for each team member:* In this approach, all team members receive the same payout, regardless of job levels, current pay, or seniority.
▶ *Different-size reward for each team member:* Using this approach, individual rewards vary based upon such factors as contribution to team results, current pay, years of experience, and skill levels of jobs performed.

How often team incentives are paid out is another important consideration. Some of the choices seen in firms with team-based incentives include payment monthly, quarterly, biannually, or annually. To reinforce the team concept, some team incentive programs allow group members to make decisions about how to allocate the team rewards to individuals.

Problems with Team Incentives

The difference between rewarding team members equally or equitably triggers many of the problems associated with team-based incentives. Rewards that are distributed in equal amounts to all team members may be perceived as unfair by employees who may work harder, have more capabilities, and perform more difficult jobs. This problem is compounded when a poorly performing individual negatively influences the team results.

In summary, it seems that the concept of people working in teams is seen as beneficial by some managers and organization leaders. But employees still expect to be paid based on individual performance, to a large extent. Until this individualism is recognized and compensation programs developed that are viewed as more equitable by more team members, caution should be used in developing and implementing team-based incentives.

Successful Team Incentives

Team incentives seem to work best when the following criteria are present:

- ▸ Significant interdependence exists among the work of several individuals, and teamwork and cooperation are essential.
- ▸ Difficulties exist in identifying exactly who is responsible for differing levels of performance.
- ▸ Management wants to create or reinforce teamwork and cooperation among employees.
- ▸ Rewards are seen as being allocated in a fair and equitable manner.
- ▸ Employee input is obtained in the design of the team-incentive plan.

If these conditions cannot be met, then either individual or organizational incentives may be more appropriate.

Gainsharing

Gainsharing is the sharing with employees of greater-than-expected gains in profits and/or productivity. Gainsharing attempts to increase "discretionary efforts"—that is, the difference between the maximum amount of effort a person can exert and the minimum amount of effort necessary to keep from being fired. Payouts of the gains can be made monthly, quarterly, semiannually, or annually, depending on management philosophy and the performance measures used. The more frequent the payouts, the greater the visibility of the rewards to employees. Therefore, given a choice, most firms with gainsharing plans have chosen to make the payouts more frequently than annually. The rewards can be distributed in four ways:

- ▸ A flat amount for all employees
- ▸ Same percentage of base salary for all employees
- ▸ Percentage of the gains by category of employees
- ▸ Amount of percentage based on individual performance against measures

ORGANIZATIONAL INCENTIVES

An organizational incentive system compensates all employees in the organization based on how well the organization as a whole performs during the year. The basic concept behind organizational incentive plans is that efficiency depends on organizational or plantwide cooperation.

Profit Sharing

As the name implies, **profit sharing** distributes a portion of organizational profits to employees. In a typical plan the percentage of the profits distributed to employees is agreed on by the end of the year before distribution. In some plans, employees receive portions of the profits at the end of the year; in others, the profits are deferred, placed in a fund, and made available to employees on retirement or on their leaving the organization.

Employee Stock Ownership Plans (ESOPs)

A common type of profit sharing is the **employee stock ownership plan (ESOP)**. An ESOP is designed to give employees stock ownership of the organization for which they work, thereby increasing their commitment, loyalty, and effort. Establishing an ESOP creates several advantages. The major one is that the firm can receive favorable tax treatment of the earnings earmarked for use in the ESOP. Second, an ESOP gives employees a "piece of the action" so that they can share in the growth and profitability of their firm. However, the sharing also can be a disadvantage because employees may feel "forced" to join, thus placing their financial future at greater risk. Both their wages or salaries and their retirement benefits depend on the performance of the organization. This concentration is even riskier for retirees because the value of their pension fund assets also depends on how well the company does. Another drawback is that ESOPs have been used as a management tool to fend off unfriendly takeover attempts.

BENEFITS

Benefits must be viewed as part of the total compensation package offered to employees. Total compensation includes money paid directly (such as wages and salaries) and money paid indirectly (such as benefits). Too often, both managers and employees think of only wages and salaries as compensation and fail to consider the significant additional costs associated with benefits expenditures.

Increasingly, employers are seeing benefits and the expenditures associated with them as linked to organizational strategic goals.[4] This linkage is especially true as one considers some of the changing demographics affecting organizations and their implications in employee benefit plans. First, employers must offer significant compensation packages if they are to compete in the tight labor markets present in many geographic locales and occupational fields. Second, the aging of the workforce places greater demands on employers to monitor the costs associated with health-care and retirement-related benefits plans. Additionally, with more dual-career couples and single-parent families, the benefits associated with work and family issues—such as family leaves, working schedules, and dependent care—are having to be addressed daily by HR professionals.

Benefits generally are not taxed as income to employees. For this reason, they may represent a somewhat more valuable reward to employees than an

FIGURE 9-3   Benefits Classified by Type

Government Mandated	Employer Voluntary

SECURITY	HEALTH CARE	FAMILY-ORIENTED
Workers' compensation	COBRA and HIPAA provisions	Family and Medical Leave Act
Unemployment compensation	Medical	Dependent care
Supplemental unemployment benefits (SUB)	Dental	Alternative work arrangements
	Vision care	**TIME OFF**
Severance pay	Prescription drugs	Military reserve time off
RETIREMENT SECURITY	Psychiatric counseling	Election and jury leaves
Social Security	Wellness programs	
Early retirement options	HMO or PPO health-care plans	Lunch and rest breaks
Preretirement counseling		Holidays and vacations
Disability retirement benefits	**FINANCIAL, INSURANCE, AND RELATED**	Funeral and bereavement leaves
Health care for retirees	Life insurance	**SOCIAL AND RECREATIONAL**
Pension plans	Legal insurance	Tennis courts
Individual retirement accounts (IRAs)	Disability insurance	Bowling leagues
401(k) and 403(b) plans	Financial counseling	Service awards
	Credit unions	Sponsored events (athletic and social)
	Company-provided car and expense account	Cafeteria and food service
	Educational assistance	Recreation programs

equivalent cash payment. Many different types of benefits are offered by employers. As Figure 9-3 indicates, some of the benefits are legally mandated by federal, state, and local laws. Employers have no choice but to pay for these benefits.

SECURITY BENEFITS

A number of benefits provide employees enhanced security. Some of these benefits are mandated by law, while others are offered by employers voluntarily. Workers' compensation, unemployment compensation, and severance pay are security benefits existing in most organizations.

Workers' compensation provides benefits to people injured on the job. State laws require most employers to provide workers' compensation coverage by purchasing insurance from a private carrier or state insurance fund or by providing self-insurance. Another benefit required by law is **unemployment compensation**, established as part of the Social Security Act of 1935. Each state operates its own unemployment compensation system, and provisions differ significantly from state to state.

Severance pay is a security benefit voluntarily offered by employers to employees who lose their jobs. Severed employees may receive lump-sum severance payments if their employment is terminated by the employer.

RETIREMENT BENEFITS

Few people have sufficient financial reserves to use when they retire, so retirement benefits attempt to provide income for employees who have retired. Except for smaller employers, most firms offer some kind of retirement plan. Generally, private pensions are a critical part of providing income for people after retirement. With the baby boomer generation closing in on retirement, pressures on such funds are likely to grow.

Pension Plans

Pension plans are retirement benefits established and funded by employers and employees. Organizations are not required to offer pension plans to employees, and many U.S. workers are not covered by them. Employers do not offer pension plans primarily because of the costs and administrative burdens imposed by government legislation.

Individual Retirement Benefit Options

The availability of several retirement benefit options makes the pension area more complex. The most prominent options are individual retirement accounts (IRAs), 401(k) and 403(b) plans, and Keogh plans. These may be available in addition to pension plans.

The **401(k) plan** gets its name from Section 401(k) of the federal tax code and is an agreement in which a percentage of an employee's pay is withheld and invested in a tax-deferred account. It allows employees to choose whether to receive cash or have employer contributions from profit-sharing and stock-bonus plans placed into tax-deferred accounts.

HEALTH-CARE BENEFITS

Employers provide a variety of health-care and medical benefits, usually through insurance coverage. The most common plans cover medical, dental, prescription drug, and vision-care expenses for employees and their dependents. Basic health-care insurance to cover both normal and major medical expenses is highly desired by employees. Dental insurance is also important to many employees. Many dental plans include orthodontic coverage, which is usually very costly. Some employer medical insurance plans also cover psychiatric counseling.

The costs of health-care insurance have escalated at a rate well in excess of inflation for several decades. However, during the last decade, employers began concerted efforts to control medical premium increases and other health-care related costs. Several approaches to restraining the growth in health-care costs are being used by employers.

Managed Care

Several types of programs are used to reduce health-care costs paid by employers. **Managed care** consists of approaches that monitor and reduce medical costs using restrictions and market system alternatives. One type of managed-care plan is the **preferred provider organization (PPO)**, a health-care provider that contracts with an employer or an employer group to provide health-care services to employees at a competitive rate. Employees have the freedom to go to other providers if they want to pay the difference in costs. A **health maintenance organization (HMO)** provides services for a fixed period on a prepaid basis. The HMO emphasizes prevention as well as correction. An employer contracts with an HMO, which has doctors and medical personnel on its staff, to furnish complete medical care, except for hospitalization.

Health-Care Legislation

The importance of health-care benefits has led to federal legislation that provides some protection to employees who leave their employers, either voluntarily or involuntarily. The two most important ones, COBRA and HIPAA, are known by the acts in which the provisions are contained.

COBRA Provisions. Legal requirements in the Consolidated Omnibus Budget Reconciliation Act (COBRA) require that most employers (except churches and the federal government) with twenty or more employees offer extended health-care coverage to the following groups:

▶ Employees who voluntarily quit, except those terminated for "gross misconduct"
▶ Widowed or divorced spouses and dependent children of former or current employees
▶ Retirees and their spouses whose health-care coverage ends

HIPAA Provisions. The Health Insurance Portability and Accountability Act (HIPAA) of 1996 allows employees to switch their health insurance plan from one company to another to get the new health coverage, regardless of preexisting health conditions. The legislation also prohibits group insurance plans from dropping coverage from a sick employee and requires them to make individual coverage available to people who leave group plans.

OTHER BENEFITS

Employers may offer workers a wide range of special benefits—financial benefits, insurance benefits (in addition to health-related insurance), educational benefits, social benefits, and recreational benefits. From the employer's point of view, such benefits can be useful in attracting and retaining employees. Workers like receiving special benefits, which are often not taxed as income.

Insurance Benefits

The most common financial-oriented benefits provided by employers are the following:

▶ Life insurance
▶ Disability insurance
▶ Legal insurance
▶ Educational benefits

Family-Oriented Benefits

The composition of families in the United States has changed significantly in the past few decades. To provide assistance, employers have established a variety of family-oriented benefits.

Family and Medical Leave Act (FMLA). Passed in 1993, the Family and Medical Leave Act (FMLA) covers all employers with fifty or more employees who live within seventy-five miles of the workplace and includes federal, state, and private employers. Only employees who have worked at least twelve months and 1,250 hours in the previous year are eligible for leaves under FMLA. The law requires that employers allow eligible employees to take a total of twelve weeks' leave during any twelve-month period for one or more of the following situations:

▶ Birth, adoption, or foster-care placement of a child
▶ Caring for a spouse, child, or parent with a serious health condition
▶ Serious health condition of the employee

Employers have had problems with the FMLA because of the many different circumstances in which employees may request and use family leave. Many employers have difficulty interpreting when and how the provisions are to be applied. Also, the need to arrange work coverage for employees on FMLA leaves can be particularly challenging for smaller employers. This difficulty is compounded because the law requires that workers on these leaves be offered similar jobs at similar levels of pay when they return to work.

Family-Care Benefits. The growing emphasis on family issues is important in many organizations for many workers. Many employers have had maternity and paternity benefits for employees upon the birth of a child. In the interest of fairness, a growing number of organizations provide benefits for employees who adopt children. Employers are addressing the child-care issue in several ways. Some organizations provide on-site day-care facilities. Other options for child-care assistance include providing referral services to aid parents in locating child-care providers and establishing discounts at day-care centers, which may be subsidized by the employer.

Another family-related issue of growing importance is caring for elderly relatives. Some responses by employers have included conducting needs surveys, providing resources, and giving referrals to elder-care providers. Some employers provide elder-care assistance through contracts with firms that arrange for elder care for employees' relatives who live elsewhere.

Benefits for Domestic Partners and Spousal Equivalents. As lifestyles have changed in the United States, employers are being confronted with requests for benefits by employees who are not married but have close personal relationships with others, such as the following:

▶ Gay and lesbian employees requesting benefits for their partners
▶ Unmarried employees who live with someone of the opposite sex

The terminology most often used to refer to individuals with such living arrangements are *domestic partners* and *spousal equivalents*. The argument made by these employees is that if an employer provides benefits for the spouses of married employees, then benefits should be provided for employees with alternative lifestyles and relationships as well.

Time-Off Benefits

Employers give employees paid time off in a variety of circumstances. Paid lunch breaks and rest periods, holidays, and vacations are the most well known. But leaves are given for a number of other purposes as well. Time-off benefits are estimated to represent from about 5% to 13% of total compensation. Some of the more common time-off benefits include holiday pay, vacation pay, and leaves of absence.

BENEFITS ADMINISTRATION

With the myriad of benefits and regulations, it is easy to see why many organizations must make coordinated efforts to administer benefits programs. The greatest role is played by HR specialists, but managers are responsible for some of the communication aspects of benefits administration.

Benefits Communication

Employees generally do not know much about the values and costs associated with the benefits they receive from employers. Yet benefits communication and benefits satisfaction are linked. Many employers have instituted special benefits communication systems to inform employees about the value of the benefits they provide.[5]

Flexible Benefits

A **flexible benefits plan**, sometimes called a *flex* or *cafeteria plan*, allows employees to select the benefits they prefer from groups of benefits established by the employer. By making a variety of "dishes," or benefits, available, the organization allows each employee to select an individual combination of benefits within some overall limits. As a result of the changing composition of the workforce, flexible benefits plans have grown in popularity.

Flexible Spending Accounts.   Under current tax laws (Section 125 of the Tax Code, administered by the Internal Revenue Service), employees can divert some income before taxes into accounts to fund certain benefits. These **flexible spending accounts** allow employees to contribute pretax dollars to buy additional benefits.

Advantages and Disadvantages of Flexible Benefits Plans.   The flexible benefits approach takes into consideration the complexity of people and situations. Because employees in an organization have different desires and needs, they can tailor benefit packages to fit their individual life situations within the limits of legal restrictions. The major problem with flexible benefits plans is the complexity of keeping track of what each individual chooses, especially if there are a large number of employees. Sophisticated computer software is now available to manage these complexities. The increase in benefits communications costs is also a concern. As more benefits are made available, employees may be less able to understand the options because the benefits structure and its provisions may become quite complicated.

NOTES

1. Peter V. LeBlanc and Paul W. Mulvey, "How American Workers See the Rewards of Work," *Compensation & Benefits Review,* January/February 1998, 24–29.

2. David J. Cichell, "Solving the Seven Riddles of Sales Compensation Design," *ACA News,* September 1998, 33–35.

3. Kisson Joseph and Manohar U. Kalwani, "The Role of Bonus Pay in Salesforce Compensation Plans," *Industrial Marketing Management* 27, 1998, 147–159.

4. Mary Ann Crowley and Virginia M. Olson, "Developing a Global Benefits Strategy," *ACA News,* January 1999, 28–30.

5. Craig Gunsauley, "So Long 'Communications,' Hello Marketing," *Employee Benefit News,* June 1998, 37–39.

SUGGESTED READINGS

Granting Stock Options, American Compensation Association, 1999.

Life Office Management Association, *401(k) Answer Book,* Panel Publishers, 1998.

Ransom and Benjamin, *Taking Family and Medical Leave,* Ransom and Benjamin, 1999.

Scott S. Rodrick, *Incentive Compensation and Employee Ownership,* The National Center for Employee Ownership, 1999.

SHRM, *Understanding HIPAA,* SHRM, 2000.

SUGGESTED INTERNET RESOURCES

Incentivecity. Shows various incentives and ways to design incentive programs.
http://www.incentivecity.com

International Foundation of Employee Benefit Plans. Contains benefits information and benefits certification details.
http://www.ifebp.org

CHAPTER 10

Employee Relations

This chapter examines several important issues in the relations of an organization with its employees. One set of issues focuses on health, safety, and security, while others address employee rights, HR policies, and discipline.

HEALTH, SAFETY, AND SECURITY

The terms *health, safety,* and *security* are closely related. The broadest and most nebulous term is <u>health</u>, which refers to a general state of physical, mental, and emotional well-being. Typically, <u>safety</u> refers to protecting the physical well-being of people. The purpose of safety programs in organizations is to prevent work-related injuries and accidents. The purpose of <u>security</u> is to protect employer facilities and equipment from unauthorized access and to protect employees while they are on work premises or work assignments. Complying with a variety of federal and state laws is fundamental for employers developing a healthy, safe, and secure workforce and working environment. A look at some major legal areas follows.

Workers' Compensation

Currently, all states have workers' compensation laws in some form. Under these laws, employers contribute to an insurance fund to compensate employees for injuries received while on the job. Premiums paid reflect the accident rate for each employer. These laws usually provide payments for lost wages, medical bills, and retraining if the worker cannot go back to the old job. Before the passage of workers' compensation laws, an employee might not recover damages for an injury, even if it was caused by hazards of the job or through the negligence of a fellow worker. Workers who died or became disabled due to occupational

FIGURE 10-1   Child Labor and Hazardous Occupations
(18 is minimum age in these occupations)

1. Manufacturing or storing explosives
2. Driving a motor vehicle and being an outside helper
3. Coal mining
4. Logging and sawmilling
5. Using power-driven woodworking machines*
6. Exposure to radioactive substances and to ionizing radiations
7. Operating power-driven hoisting apparatus
8. Operating power-driven, metal-forming, punching, and shearing machines*
9. Mining, other than coal mining
10. Slaughtering, or meat packing, processing, or rendering*
11. Using power-driven bakery machines
12. Operating power-driven paper products machines*
13. Manufacturing brick, tile, and related products
14. Using power-driven circular saws, and guillotine shears*
15. Wrecking, demolition, and ship-breaking operations
16. Roofing operations*
17. Excavation operations*

*In certain cases, the law provides exemptions for apprentices and student learners in these occupations

Source: Employment Standards Administration, Wage and Hour Division, U.S. Department of Labor, *Child Labor Requirements in Nonagricultural Occupations,* WH Publication no. 1330 (Washington, DC: U.S. Government Printing Office).

injury or disease received no financial guarantees for their families. Employers (and society) assumed that safety was the employee's responsibility.

Workers' compensation costs have increased dramatically in the past and have become a major issue in many states. These costs represent from 2% to 10% of payroll for most employers. Only recently has there been a small decline as workplaces have become safer and management has begun to manage workers' compensation programs to hold costs down.[1]

Child Labor Laws

Another area of safety concern is reflected in restrictions affecting younger workers, especially those under age 18. Child labor laws, found in Section XII of the Fair Labor Standards Act (FLSA), set the minimum age for most employment at 16 years. For "hazardous" occupations, 18 years is the minimum. Figure 10-1 shows occupations that are considered hazardous by the government.

Americans with Disabilities Act

The Americans with Disabilities Act (ADA) is an entirely new form of regulation for health and safety. The ADA has created some problems for employers. For example, employers sometimes try to return injured workers to "light-duty" work in order to reduce workers' compensation costs. However, under the ADA, in making accommodations for injured employees through light-duty work, employers may be undercutting what really are *essential job functions*. Making such accommodations for injured employees for extended periods of time may require an employer to make accommodations for all job applicants with disabilities.

OCCUPATIONAL SAFETY AND HEALTH ACT *OSHA*

The Occupational Safety and Health Act of 1970 was passed "to assure so far as possible every working man or woman in the Nation safe and healthful working conditions and to preserve our human resources." Every employer engaged in commerce who has one or more employees is covered by the act. Farmers having fewer than ten employees are exempt. Employers in specific industries, such as coal mining, are covered under other health and safety acts. Federal, state, and local government employees also are covered by separate provisions or statutes.

OSHA has fewer than a thousand inspectors for the entire country. With over six million workplaces to visit, some kind of priority system must be established. Inspection is aimed most frequently at sites having significantly higher-than-industry-average injury and illness records.

The Occupational Health and Safety Act requires that in areas in which no standards have been adopted, the employer has a *general duty* to provide safe and healthy working conditions. Employers who know of, or who should reasonably know of, unsafe or unhealthy conditions can be cited for violating the general-duty clause. Also, employers are responsible for knowing about and informing their employees of safety and health standards established by OSHA, and for displaying OSHA posters in prominent places.

OSHA Inspections

The Occupational Safety and Health Act provides for on-the-spot inspections by OSHA representatives, called *compliance officers* or *inspectors*. While OSHA inspectors can issue citations for violations of the provisions of the act, whether a citation is issued depends on the severity and extent of the problems and on the employer's knowledge of them. In addition, depending on the nature and number of violations, penalties can be assessed against employers. The nature and extent of the penalties depend on the type and severity of the violations as determined by OSHA officials.

Record-Keeping Requirements

OSHA has established a standard national system for recording occupational injuries, accidents, and fatalities. Employers are generally required to maintain a detailed annual record of the various types of accidents for inspection by OSHA representatives and for submission to the agency. Employers that have had good safety records in previous years and with fewer than ten employees are not required to keep detailed records. However, many organizations must complete OSHA Form 200. The following organizations are required to complete OSHA 200 reports:

▶ Firms having frequent hospitalizations, injuries, or illnesses
▶ Firms having work-related deaths
▶ Firms included in OSHA's annual labor statistics survey

No one knows how many industrial accidents go unreported. It may be many more than anyone suspects, despite the fact that OSHA has increased its surveillance of accident-reporting records.

Accident frequency and severity rates must be calculated. Regulations from OSHA require organizations to calculate injury frequency rates per hundred full-time employees on an annual basis. Employers compute accident severity rates by figuring the number of lost-time cases, the number of lost workdays, and the number of deaths. These figures are then related to total work hours per hundred full-time employees and compared with industrywide rates and other employers' rates.

Four types of injuries or illnesses have been defined by the Occupational Safety and Health Act:

▶ *Injury- or illness-related deaths*
▶ *Lost-time or disability injuries:* These include job-related injuries or disabling occurrences that cause an employee to miss his or her regularly scheduled work on the day following the accident.
▶ *Medical-care injuries:* These injuries require treatment by a physician but do not cause an employee to miss a regularly scheduled work turn.
▶ *Minor injuries:* These injuries require first-aid treatment and do not cause an employee to miss the next regularly scheduled work turn.

Evaluating the Effects of OSHA

By making employers and employees more aware of safety and health considerations, OSHA has had a significant impact on organizations. But how effective the act has been is not clear. It does appear that OSHA regulations have reduced the number of accidents and injuries in some cases. But while some studies have shown that OSHA has had a positive impact, others have shown that OSHA has had no impact.

FIGURE 10-2   **Approaches to Effective Safety Management**

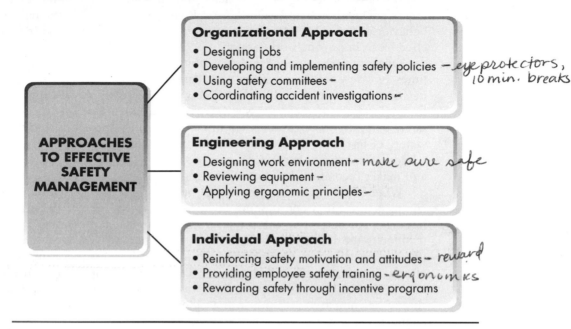

APPROACHES TO EFFECTIVE SAFETY MANAGEMENT

Organizational Approach
- Designing jobs
- Developing and implementing safety policies — *eye protectors,*
- Using safety committees — *10 min. breaks*
- Coordinating accident investigations —

Engineering Approach
- Designing work environment — *make sure safe*
- Reviewing equipment —
- Applying ergonomic principles —

Individual Approach
- Reinforcing safety motivation and attitudes — *reward*
- Providing employee safety training — *ergonomics*
- Rewarding safety through incentive programs

SAFETY MANAGEMENT

Effective safety management requires an organizational commitment to safe working conditions. But as important, well-designed and well-managed safety programs can pay dividends in reduced accidents and associated costs, such as workers' compensation and possible fines.

Components of Effective Safety Management Programs

Effective safety management programs usually contain the following:

- ▶ Organizational commitment and responsibility
- ▶ Safety policies and discipline
- ▶ Safety training and communications
- ▶ Safety committees
- ▶ Inspection, accident investigation, and research
- ▶ Evaluation of safety efforts

At the heart of safety management is an organizational commitment to a comprehensive safety effort. This effort should be coordinated from the top level of management to include all members of the organization. There are three different approaches that an employer might choose in managing safety. Successful programs may use all three in dealing with safety issues. Figure 10-2 shows the organizational, engineering, and individual approaches and their components. Designing safety policies and rules and disciplining violators are important components of safety efforts. Frequently reinforcing the need for safe behavior and supplying feedback on positive safety practices also are extremely effective in improving worker safety.

One way to encourage employee safety is to involve all employees at various times in safety training sessions and committee meetings and to have these meetings frequently. In addition to safety training, continuous communication to develop safety consciousness is necessary. Workers frequently are involved in safety planning through safety committees, often composed of workers from a variety of levels and departments. A safety committee generally has regularly scheduled meetings, has specific responsibilities for conducting safety reviews, and makes recommendations for changes necessary to avoid future accidents.

When accidents occur, they should be investigated by the employer's safety committee or safety coordinator. In investigating the *scene* of an accident, it is important to determine the physical and environmental conditions that contributed to the accident. Poor lighting, poor ventilation, and wet floors are some possible contributors. Organizations should monitor and evaluate their safety efforts. Just as organizational accounting records are audited, a firm's safety efforts should be audited periodically as well. Accident and injury statistics should be compared with previous accident patterns to identify any significant changes.

ISSUES IN SAFETY AND HEALTH

Logic and reason suggest that both work design and human work behaviors contribute to safety. Yet some approaches to reducing accidents focus on one or the other exclusively. Both approaches as part of a well-organized safety effort are valuable, so they tend to be most effective when considered jointly.

Designing jobs properly requires consideration of the physical setting of a job. The way the work space surrounding a job is used can influence the worker's performance of the job itself. Several factors relating to the physical settings of jobs have been identified, including the size of the work area, kinds of materials used, sensory conditions, distance between work areas, and interference from noise and traffic flow. Temperature, noise, and light levels are sensory conditions that affect job performance.

The Environmental Protection Agency (EPA) defines *sick building syndrome* as a situation in which occupants experience acute health problems and discomfort that appear to be linked to time spent in a building. One cause of sick buildings is poor air quality, which occurs with "sealed" buildings where windows cannot be opened. Inadequate ventilation, as well as airborne contamination from carpets, molds, copy machines, adhesives, and fungi, can cause sick buildings. Also, problems may result when the air flow and circulation controls are too sophisticated for the people who maintain them, or when operators try to cut corners to save energy.

✳   **Ergonomics** is the proper design of the work environment to address the physical demands experienced by people. The term comes from the Greek *ergon,* meaning "work," and the suffix *-omics,* meaning "management of." An ergonomist studies physiological, psychological, and engineering design aspects of a job, including such factors as fatigue, lighting, tools, equipment layout, and placement of controls. *Human factors engineering* is a related field.

Employers can prevent some accidents by designing machines, equipment, and work areas so that workers who daydream periodically or who perform potentially dangerous jobs cannot injure themselves and others. Providing safety equipment and guards on machinery and installing emergency switches often forestall accidents.

Repetitive stress injuries, repetitive motion injuries, cumulative trauma disorders, carpal tunnel syndrome, ergonomic hazards—this listing of serious-sounding problems applies to many workplaces. **Cumulative trauma disorders (CTDs)** occur when workers repetitively use the same muscles to perform tasks, resulting in muscle and skeletal injuries. These problems are occurring in a variety of work settings. The meatpacking industry has the highest level of CTDs. But office workers increasingly are experiencing CTDs, primarily from extensive typing and data entry on computers and computer-related equipment.

Individuals and Safety

Engineers approach safety from the perspective of redesigning the machinery or the work area. Industrial psychologists see safety differently. They are concerned with the proper match of individuals to jobs and emphasize employee training in safety methods, fatigue reduction, and health awareness.

Industrial psychologists have conducted numerous field studies with thousands of employees, looking at the "human factors" in accidents. The results show a definite relationship between emotional factors, such as stress, and accidents. Other studies point to the importance of individual differences, motivation, attitudes, and learning as key factors in controlling the human element in safety. The individual-based safety approach attempts to identify and modify behaviors that can lead to accidents.[2] It may use "coaches" or "observers" to identify dangerous behavior.

Work schedules can be another cause for accidents. The relationship between work schedules and accidents can be explained as follows: Fatigue based on physical exertion rarely exists in today's industrial workplace. But fatigue defined as boredom, which occurs when a person is required to do the same tasks for a long period of time, is rather common. As fatigue of this kind increases, motivation is reduced; along with decreased motivation, workers' attention wanders, and the likelihood of accidents increases.

Persuading employees to keep safety standards continuously in mind while performing their jobs is difficult. Often, employees think that safety measures are bothersome and unnecessary until an injury occurs. For example, it may be necessary for employees to wear safety glasses in a laboratory most of the time.

But if the glasses are awkward, employees may resist using them, even when they know they should have protection. To encourage employees to work safely, many organizations have used safety contests and have given employees incentives for safe work behavior. Unfortunately, there is some evidence that incentives tend to reinforce underreporting and "creative" classifying of accidents. In the last few days of a big safety contest, most people will think long and hard before they cost their team the prize by reporting an accident.[3]

HEALTH

Employee health problems are varied—and somewhat inevitable. They can range from minor illnesses such as colds to serious illnesses related to the jobs performed. Some employees have emotional health problems; others have alcohol or drug problems. Some problems are chronic; others are transitory. But all may affect organizational operations and individual employee productivity.

Employers are increasingly confronted by problems associated with employees who have AIDS or other life-threatening illnesses such as cancer. There is an eventual decline in productivity and attendance brought on by progressive deterioration. Then, with AIDS specifically, there are the problems associated with co-worker anxiety in the workplace. It appears that many companies deem it unnecessary to adopt specific policies that deal with AIDS and other life-threatening illnesses because they do not want to draw attention to them and unnecessarily alarm employees. No matter what information the experts might offer to assuage the fear of other employees, a co-worker with AIDS, whether on the shop floor or in the executive offices, creates feelings of anxiety and unease among other employees, suppliers, and customers.

Smoking at Work

Arguments and rebuttals characterize the smoking-at-work controversy, and statistics are rampant. A multitude of state and local laws have been passed that deal with smoking in the workplace and public places. Passage of these laws has been viewed by many employers positively, because they relieve employers of the responsibility for making decisions on smoking issues. But many courts, unlike state legislatures, have been hesitant to address the smoking-at-work issue. They clearly prefer to let employers and employees resolve their differences rather than prohibiting or supporting the right to smoke.

Substance Abuse

Substance abuse is defined as the use of illicit substances or the misuse of controlled substances, alcohol, or other drugs. The millions of substance abusers in the workforce cost the United States billions of dollars annually.

Drug tests are used by many employers, and the number of positive test results are dropping. These results may mean that fewer employees are using drugs, or that drug users have learned to avoid analysis, or both. If an employee tests positive the first time, 22% of employers terminate that worker immediately, 21% take disciplinary actions, and 63% refer the worker to counseling and treatment.[4] Alcohol testing is on the rise as well; about a third of businesses test for alcohol use. Most such testing follows an accident or is done for reasonable cause, such as failing a fitness-for-duty test.[5]

The Americans with Disabilities Act (ADA) determines how management can handle substance abuse cases. The practicing illegal drug abuser is specifically excluded from the definition of disabled under the act. However, those addicted to legal substances (alcohol, for example) are not excluded. Previous legislation and various government agencies have defined *disabled* differently, but members of the medical community seem to agree that both alcohol and drug abuse are mental disorders.

Employers are concerned about substance abuse because it alters work behaviors. The effects may be subtle, such as tardiness, increased absenteeism, slower work pace, higher rate of mistakes, and less time spent at the workstation. Substance abuse also can cause altered behaviors at work, so that more withdrawal (physical and psychological) and antagonistic behaviors occur. Also, the organization may be held liable for injuries to others if its managers should have been aware that an employee's drug use was a problem. Employers who are concerned about maintaining a healthy workforce must move beyond simply providing healthy working conditions and begin to address employee health and wellness in other ways.

Wellness Programs

Employers' desires to improve productivity, decrease absenteeism, and control health-care costs have come together in the "wellness" movement. **Wellness programs** are designed to maintain or improve employee health before problems arise. Wellness programs encourage self-directed lifestyle changes. Early wellness programs were aimed primarily at reducing the cost and risk of disease. Newer programs emphasize healthy lifestyles and environment. Typical programs may include the following:

- ▶ Screenings for risk factors (blood pressures, cardiovascular disease, etc.)
- ▶ Exercise programs (endurance, aerobics, strength, etc.)
- ▶ Education and awareness programs (stress reduction, weight control, prevention of back pain, etc.)
- ▶ Skills programs (CPR, first aid, etc.)

Employee Assistance Programs (EAPs)

One method that organizations are using as a broad-based response to health issues is the **employee assistance program (EAP)**, which provides counseling and other help to employees having emotional, physical, or other personal problems. In such a program, an employer establishes a liaison with a social service counseling agency. Employees who have problems may then contact the agency, either voluntarily or by employer referral, for assistance with a broad range of problems. Counseling costs are paid for by the employer, either in total or up to a preestablished limit.

SECURITY

A shocking statistic is that *homicide* is the second leading cause of workplace fatalities in the United States, following only transportation-related deaths. Workers such as police officers, taxi drivers, and convenience store clerks are more likely to be murdered on the job than employees in many other occupations. Often, these deaths occur during armed robbery attempts. But what has shocked many employers in a variety of industries has been how many disgruntled employees or former employees have resorted to homicide in the workplace to deal with their anger and grievances. These concerns have led many employers to conduct training for supervisors and managers on how to recognize the signs of a potentially violent employee and what to do when violence occurs. During training at many firms, supervisors learn the typical profile of potentially violent employees. Violence that begins at home with family or "friends" can spill over to the workplace. Women are much more likely than men to experience violence committed as a result of a personal relationship. The same is true in the workplace. On the other hand, men are more likely to be attacked by a stranger.

Conducting a comprehensive analysis of the vulnerability of organizational security is the purpose of a **security audit**. Often, such an audit uses managers inside the organization—such as the HR manager and facilities manager—and outsiders, such as security consultants, police officers, fire officials, and computer security experts.

A key aspect of security is controlling access to the physical facilities of the organization. As mentioned earlier, many workplace homicides occur during robberies. Therefore, those employees most vulnerable, such as taxi drivers and convenience store clerks, must be provided secure areas to which access is limited.

Another important aspect of providing security is to screen job applicants. As discussed earlier, there are legal limits on what can be done, particularly regarding the use of psychological tests and checking of references. However, firms that do not adequately screen employees may be subject to liability if an employee commits crimes later.

Employees come to organizations with certain rights that have been established by the U.S. constitution. Some of those rights include *freedom of speech, due process,* protection against *unreasonable search and seizure,* and others. Although the U.S. Constitution grants these and other rights to citizens, over the years laws and court decisions have identified limits on those rights in the workplace.

EMPLOYEE RIGHTS AND RESPONSIBILITIES

Federal, state, and local laws that grant employees certain rights at work, such as equal employment opportunity, collective bargaining, and safety have changed traditional management prerogatives. These laws and their interpretations have been the subjects of a considerable number of court cases. An employee's **contractual rights** are based on a specific contractual agreement with an employer. Details of an employment agreement are often spelled out in a formal employment contract. These contracts are written and often very detailed. Traditionally, employment contracts have been used mostly for executives and senior managers. However, the use of employment contracts is filtering down the organization to include scarce-skilled, highly specialized professionals and technical employees.

The idea that a contract (even an implied, unwritten one) exists between workers and their employers affects the employment relationship. Rights and responsibilities of the employee to the employer may be spelled out in a job description, in an employment contract, or in HR policies, but often are not. Employee rights and responsibilities also may exist only as unwritten employer expectations about what is acceptable behavior or performance on the part of the employee.

Workplace litigation has reached epidemic proportions as employees who feel that their rights have been violated sue their employers. Some employers are purchasing insurance to try to cover their risks from numerous lawsuits. As employees increasingly regard themselves as free agents in the workplace—and as the power of unions declines—the struggle between employee and employer "rights" is heightening. Employers frequently do not fare very well in court. Further, it is not only the employer that is liable in many cases. Individual managers and supervisors have been found liable if hiring or promotion decisions have been based on discriminatory factors, or when they have had knowledge of such conduct and have not taken steps to stop it.

RIGHTS AFFECTING THE EMPLOYMENT RELATIONSHIP

It can be argued that all employee-rights issues affect the employment relationship. However, several basic issues predominate: employment-at-will, due process, and dismissal for just cause.

Employment-at-Will (EAW)

Employment-at-will (EAW) is a common-law doctrine stating that employers have the right to hire, fire, demote, or promote whomever they choose, unless there is a law or contract to the contrary. In the past three decades an increasing number of state courts have questioned the fairness of an employer's decision to fire an employee without just cause and due process. Many lawsuits have stressed that employees have job rights that must be balanced against EAW.

Employers who violate EAW restrictive statutes may be found guilty of **wrongful discharge**, which occurs when an employer terminates an individual's employment for reasons that are illegal or improper. Some state courts have recognized certain nonstatutory grounds for wrongful-discharge suits. Additionally, courts generally have held that unionized workers cannot pursue EAW actions as at-will employees because they are covered by the grievance/arbitration process.

Wrongful-discharge lawsuits have become a major concern for many firms. According to a study, the median compensatory award for wrongful-termination cases lost by employers was $204,310. The same study found that wrongfully discharged executives won their cases 58% of the time, but general laborers won only 42% of their cases.[6]

Just Cause

What constitutes **just cause** as sufficient justification for employment-related actions such as dismissal usually is spelled out in union contracts, but often is not as clear in at-will situations. While the definition of just cause varies, the criteria used by courts have become well-defined.

Just cause determinants are as follows:

- ▶ Was the employee warned of the consequences of the conduct?
- ▶ Was the employer's rule reasonable?
- ▶ Did management investigate before disciplining?
- ▶ Was the investigation fair and impartial?
- ▶ Was there evidence of guilt?
- ▶ Were the rules and penalties applied in an evenhanded fashion?
- ▶ Was the penalty reasonable, given the offense?

Due Process

In employment settings, **due process** is the opportunity for individuals to explain and defend their actions against charges of misconduct or other reasons. Certain factors usually must be addressed by HR managers and employers if due process procedures are to be perceived as fair by the courts:

- ▶ How have precedents been handled?
- ▶ Is a complaint process available?
- ▶ Was the complaint process used?
- ▶ Was retaliation used against the employee?
- ▶ Was a decision made based on facts?
- ▶ Were the actions and processes viewed as fair by outside entities?

Some employers allow employees to appeal disciplinary actions to an internal committee of employees. This **peer review panel** is composed of employees who

[handwritten note in left margin: The right to face the accuser & defend themselves]

[handwritten note at bottom: must go through grievance policy before anything. meet timelines]

hear appeals from disciplined employees and make recommendations or decisions. In general, such panels reverse management decisions much less often than might be expected.

BALANCING EMPLOYER SECURITY CONCERNS AND EMPLOYEE RIGHTS

The **right to privacy** that individuals have is defined in legal terms as the freedom from unauthorized and unreasonable intrusion into their personal affairs. Although the right to privacy is not specifically identified in the U.S. Constitution, a number of past Supreme Court cases have established that such a right must be considered.

The growing use of technology in organizations is making it more difficult to balance employer security rights with employee privacy concerns. Although computers, cameras, and telecommunications systems are transforming many workplaces, the use of these items by employers to monitor employee actions is raising concerns that the privacy rights of employees are being threatened.

Individuals who report real or perceived wrongs committed by their employers are called **whistle-blowers**. Two key questions in regard to whistle-blowing are (1) When do employees have the right to speak out with protection from retribution?; and (2) When do employees violate the confidentiality of their jobs by speaking out? Often, the answers are difficult to determine. What is clear is that retaliation against whistle-blowers is not allowed, based on a number of court decisions.

Monitoring of E-Mail and Voice Mail

Both e-mail and voice-mail systems increasingly are seen by employers as areas where employers have a right to monitor what is said and transmitted. Technological advances in information and telecommunications have became a major issue for employers regarding employee privacy. The use of e-mail and voice mail increases every day, also raising employers' risk of being liable if they monitor or inspect employee electronic communications.[7]

Federal constitutional rights, such as the right to protection from unreasonable search and seizure, protect an individual only against the activities of the government. Thus, employees of both private-sector and government employers can be monitored, observed, and searched at work by representatives of the employer. This principle has been reaffirmed by several court decisions, which have held that both private-sector and government employers may search desks and files without search warrants if they believe that work rules have been violated. Often, workplace searches and surveillance are used as part of employee performance monitoring. Employee performance may be monitored to measure performance, ensure performance quality and customer service, check for theft, or enforce company rules or laws. Performance monitoring occurs with truck drivers, nurses, teleservice customer service representatives, and many other jobs.

FIGURE 10-3 **Methods of Reducing Employee Theft**

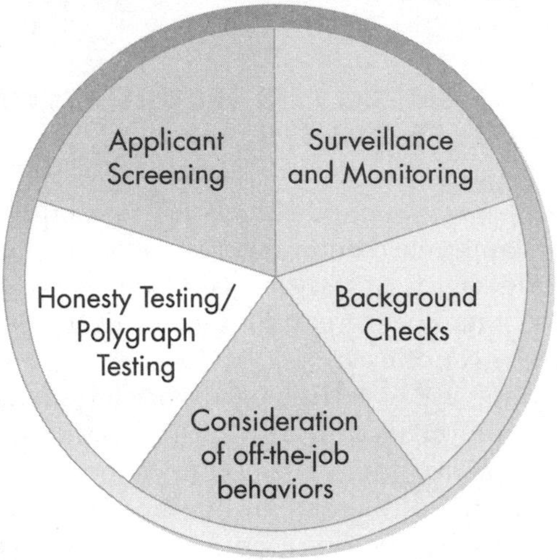

The common concern in a monitored workplace is usually not whether monitoring should be used, but how it should be conducted, how the information should be used, and how feedback should be communicated to employees.

As a minimum, employers should obtain a signed employee consent form indicating that performance monitoring and taping of phone calls will occur. Also, employers should communicate that monitoring is done and will be done regularly.

Video Surveillance

Numerous employers have installed video surveillance systems in workplaces. Sometimes these video systems are used to ensure employee security, such as in parking lots, garages, and dimly lighted exterior areas. Other employers have installed them in retail sales floors, production areas, parts and inventory rooms, and lobbies. But it is when video surveillance is extended into employee restrooms, changing rooms, and other more private areas that employer rights and employee privacy collide.

An increasing problem faced by employers is theft of employer property and vital company secrets. Figure 10-3 shows methods used to reduce employee theft.

The Drug-Free Workplace Act of 1988

The U.S. Supreme Court has ruled that certain drug testing plans do not violate the Constitution. But private employer programs are governed mainly by state laws, which currently are a confusing hodgepodge. Passage of the Drug-Free Workplace Act in 1988 has required government contractors to take steps to eliminate employee drug use. Failure to do so can lead to contract termination. Tobacco and alcohol are not considered controlled substances under the act, and off-the-job drug use is not included.

It is interesting to note that employee attitudes toward drug testing appear to have changed. Apparently, experience with workplace drug problems has made managers and employees less tolerant of drug users. Drug testing appears to be most acceptable to employees when they see the procedures being used as fair, and when characteristics of the job (such as danger to other people) require that the employee be alert and fully functioning.

The most common tests for drug use are urinalysis, radioimmunoassay of hair, and fitness-for-duty testing. Urinalysis is the test most frequently used. It requires a urine sample that must be tested at a lab. There is concern about sample switching, and the test detects drug use only over the past few days. But urinalysis is generally accurate and well accepted.

HR POLICIES, PROCEDURES, AND RULES

Where there is a choice among actions, **policies** act as general guidelines that focus organizational actions. Policies are general in nature, while procedures and rules are specific to the situation.

Procedures are customary methods of handling activities and are more specific than policies. For example, a *policy* may state that employees will be given vacations. *Procedures* then establish a specific method for authorizing vacation time without disrupting work.

Rules are specific guidelines that regulate and restrict the behavior of individuals. They are similar to procedures in that they guide action and typically allow no discretion in their application. Rules reflect a management decision that action be taken—or not taken—in a given situation.

Guidelines for an Employee Handbook

An employee handbook gives employees a reference source for company policies and rules and can be a positive tool for effective management of human resources. Even smaller organizations can prepare handbooks relatively easily using computer software. There is a current legal trend to use employee handbooks against employers in lawsuits charging a broken "implied" contract. But that is no reason to abandon employee handbooks as a way to communicate policies to employees. Not having an employee handbook with HR policies spelled out can also leave an organization open to costly litigation and out-of-court settlements.

A more sensible approach is first to develop sound HR policies and employee handbooks to communicate them and then have legal counsel review the language contained in them. Recommendations include the following:

▶ Eliminate controversial phrases.
▶ Use disclaimers.
▶ Keep the handbook current.

[handwritten note in left margin: if you need to get rid of someone, get rid of them. Don't let them hang on.]

EMPLOYEE DISCIPLINE

Employee rights are linked to employee discipline because employee rights are often an issue in disciplinary cases. **Discipline** is a form of training that enforces organizational rules. Those most often affected by the discipline systems in an organization are problem employees. Fortunately, problem employees constitute a small number of employees, but they often are the ones who cause the most difficult situations. If employers fail to deal with problem employees, negative effects on other employees and work groups often result.

Approaches to Discipline

The disciplinary system can be viewed as an application of behavior modification for problem or unproductive employees. The best discipline is clearly self-discipline; when most people understand what is required at work, they can usually be counted on to do their jobs effectively. Yet some find that the prospect of external discipline helps their self-discipline. This philosophy has led to the development of the positive discipline approach.

Positive Discipline Approach. The positive discipline approach builds on the philosophy that violations are actions that can be constructively corrected without penalty. In this approach, the focus is on fact finding and guidance to encourage desirable behaviors, instead of on using penalties to discourage undesirable behaviors.

Progressive Discipline Approach. Progressive discipline incorporates a sequence of steps into the shaping of employee behaviors. Figure 10-4 shows a typical progressive discipline system. Like the procedures in the figure, most progressive discipline procedures use verbal and written reprimands and suspension before resorting to dismissal. Thus, progressive discipline suggests that actions to modify behavior become progressively more severe as the employee continues to show improper behavior.

Discharge: The Final Disciplinary Step. A manager may feel guilty when dismissing an employee, and sometimes guilt is justified. If an employee fails, it may be because the manager was not able to create an appropriate work environment. Perhaps the employee was not adequately trained, or perhaps management failed to establish effective policies. Managers are responsible for their employees, and to an extent, they share the blame for failures.

FIGURE 10-4   Progressive Discipline Procedure

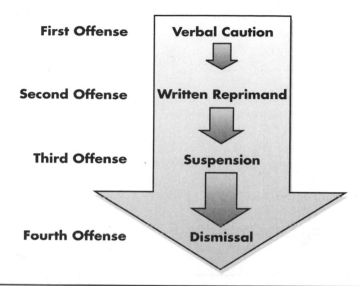

First Offense — Verbal Caution

Second Offense — Written Reprimand

Third Offense — Suspension

Fourth Offense — Dismissal

NOTES

1. Kristin Grimsley, "Workers' Compensation Costs, Payments Down," *The Washington Post,* December 19, 1997, G3
2. E. Scott Geller, "Behavior-Based Safety: Confusion, Controversy, and Clarification," *Occupational Health & Safety,* January 1999, 40–49.
3. Tom Krause and Stan Hodson, "A Close Look at Safety Incentives," *Occupational Health & Safety,* January 1998, 28.
4. Jane Bahls, "Drugs in the Workplace," *HR Magazine,* February 1998, 81–87.
5. "Employee Alcohol Testing on the Rise," *Bulletin to Management,* August 20, 1998, 261.
6. Jay Stiller, "You'll Be Hearing from My Lawyer," *Across the Board,* January 1997, 32–38.
7. Susan Peticolas and Kerrie R. Heslin, "Electronic Communications in the Workplace," *Legal Report,* Winter 1999, 5–8; and Brenda Paik Sunoo, "What If Your E-Mail Ends Up in Court?" *Workforce,* July 1998, 36–41.

SUGGESTED READINGS

Nancy Campbell, *Writing Effective Policies and Procedures,* AMACOM, 1998.

Mark Moran, *The OSHA Answer Book,* Moran Associates, 1999.

Fred S. Steingold, *The Employer's Legal Handbook,* 2nd ed., Nolo Press, 1998.

Donald H. Weiss, *Fair, Square, and Legal,* AMACOM, 1999.

SUGGESTED INTERNET RESOURCES

OSHA. Information from the U.S. Occupational Safety and Health Administration.
http://www.osha.gov

Privacy & American Business. Describes the organizational resources and programs.
http://www.pandab.org

11

Union-Management Relations

When employees have chosen to be represented by a labor union, a number of laws must be considered. The nature of union-management relations affects how HR management is practiced.

A union is a formal association of workers that promotes the interests of its members through collective action. The state of unions varies among countries depending on the culture and laws that define union-management relationships. In the United States a complex system of laws, administrative agencies, and precedent is in place to allow workers to join unions when they wish to do so. Although fewer workers choose to do so today than before, the mechanisms remain for a union resurgence if employees feel they need a formal representative to deal with management. This chapter examines why employees may choose to join a union, how they go about it, and the bargaining and administration of the agreement that union and management reach.

WHEN MANAGEMENT FACES A UNION

Employers usually would rather not have to deal with a union. The wages paid union workers are higher, and unions constrain what managers can and cannot do in a number of HR areas. However, unions *can be* associated with higher productivity, although that may occur when management has to find labor-saving ways of doing work to offset higher wage costs. Some firms pursue a strategy of good relations with unions. Others may choose an aggressive, adversarial approach; this is especially true among companies that follow a low-cost/low-wage strategy to deal with competition.

Why Employees Unionize

Whether a union targets a group of employees, or the employees themselves request union assistance, the union still must win sufficient support from the employees if it is to become their legal representative. Research consistently shows that employees join unions for one primary reason: they are dissatisfied with how they are treated by their employers and feel the union can improve the situation. If the employees do not get organizational justice from their employers, they turn to the union to assist them in getting what they believe is equitable. Important factors seem to be *wages and benefits, job security,* and *supervisory treatment.*

The primary determinant of whether employees unionize is management. If management treats employees like valuable human resources, then employees generally feel no need for outside representation. That is why providing good working conditions, fair treatment by supervisors, responsiveness to worker complaints and concerns, and reasonably competitive wages and benefits are all antidotes to unionization efforts. In addition, many workers want more cooperative dealings with management, rather than being autocratically managed.[1] The union's ability to foster commitment from members and to remain as their bargaining agent apparently depends on how well the union succeeds in providing services that its members want.

UNIONS IN THE UNITED STATES

The union movement in the United States has been characterized by the following key approaches, which in some cases are very different from the approaches used in other countries:

- ▶ *Focus on economic issues:* Unions typically have focused on improving the "bread and butter" issues for their members—wages, job security, and benefits.
- ▶ *Organized by type of job:* In the United States, carpenters often belong to the carpenter's union, truck drivers to the Teamsters, and teachers to the American Federation of Teachers or the National Education Association.
- ▶ *Decentralized bargaining:* In the United States, bargaining is usually done on a company-by-company basis, rather than setting nationwide rates through bargaining.
- ▶ *Collective agreements as contracts:* Collective bargaining agreements are referred to as contracts. They spell out work rules and conditions of employment for two or three years or longer. In the United States, the agreements are enforceable after interpretation (if necessary) by an arbitrator.
- ▶ *Adversarial relations:* U.S. tradition has management and labor as adversaries who must "clash" to reach agreement.

FIGURE 11-1   **Union Membership as a Percentage of U.S. Workforce**

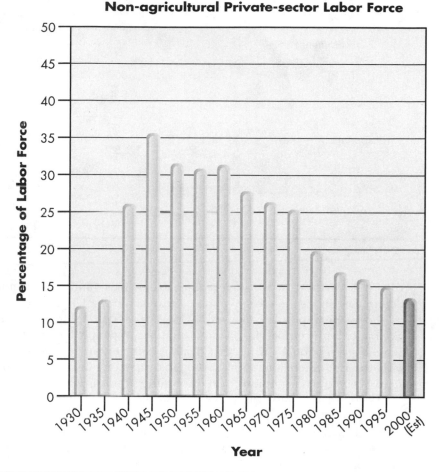

Non-agricultural Private-sector Labor Force

Source: Data from Bureau of Labor Statistics, U.S. Department of Labor.

Union Decline Worldwide

Over the past several decades, the statistics on union membership have told a disheartening story for organized labor in the United States. As shown in Figure 11-1, unions represented over 30% of the workforce from 1945 through 1960. But by the end of the 1990s, unions in the United States represented less than 14% of all private-sector workers.

As in the United States, unions in other countries are facing declining membership. One factor in the decline of European unions is that European manufacturers have been reducing operations in Europe and moving jobs to the

FIGURE 11-2 Percentage of Workers in Unions, by Industry

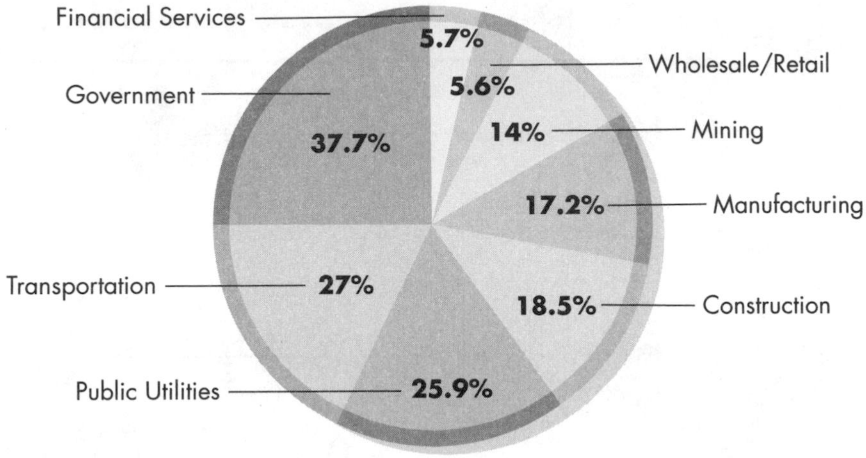

Source: Data from Bureau of Labor Statistics, U.S. Department of Labor.

United States and to low-wage countries such as China, Thailand, and the Philippines, in part to escape union constraints in the United States.

Economists speculate that several issues have sparked union decline: deregulation, foreign competition, a larger number of people looking for jobs, and a general perception by firms that dealing with unions is expensive compared with the nonunion alternative. Also, management has taken a much more activist stance against unions than during the previous years of union growth.

Unions have emphasized helping workers obtain higher wages, shorter working hours, job security, and safe working conditions from their employers. Ironically, some believe that one cause for the decline of unions has been their success in getting their important worker issues passed into law for everyone. Therefore, unions are not as necessary for many employees, even though they enjoy the results of past union efforts to influence legislation.

Public-Sector Unionism

An area where unions have had some measure of success is with public-sector employees, particularly with state and local government workers. Figure 11-2 shows that the government sector (federal, state, and local) is the most highly unionized part of the U.S. workforce.

Unionization of state and local government employees presents some unique problems and challenges. Many unionized local government employees are in critical service areas. Allowing police officers, firefighters, and sanitation workers to strike endangers public health and safety. Consequently, more than thirty states have laws prohibiting public employee work stoppages. These laws also identify a variety of ways to resolve negotiation impasses, including arbitration. But unions still give employees in these areas greater security and better ability to influence decisions on wages and benefits.

THE HISTORY OF AMERICAN UNIONS

The evolution of the union movement in the United States began with early collective efforts by employees to address job concerns and counteract management power. As early as 1794, shoemakers organized a union, picketed, and conducted strikes. However, in those days, unions in the United States received very little support from the courts. In 1806, when the shoemakers' union struck for higher wages, a Philadelphia court found union members guilty of engaging in a "criminal conspiracy" to raise wages.

In 1886, the American Federation of Labor (AFL) was formed as a federation of independent national unions. Its aims were to organize skilled craft workers, such as carpenters and plumbers, and to emphasize such bread-and-butter issues as wages and working conditions. The Civil War gave factories a big boost, and factory mass-production methods used semiskilled or unskilled workers. Unions found that they could not control the semiskilled workers entering factory jobs because these workers had no tradition of unionism. It was not until 1938, when the Congress of Industrial Organizations (CIO) was founded, that a labor union organization focused on semiskilled and unskilled workers. Years later, the AFL and the CIO merged to form one coordinating federation, the AFL-CIO.

The right to organize workers and engage in collective bargaining is of little value if workers are not free to exercise it. Historical evidence shows that management developed practices calculated to prevent workers from using this right. The federal government has taken action over time both to hamper unions and to protect them.

THE "NATIONAL LABOR CODE"

The economic crises of the early 1930s and the restrictions on workers' ability to organize into unions led to the passage of landmark labor legislation. Later acts reflected other pressures and issues that had to be addressed legislatively. Together, the following three acts, passed over a period of almost 25 years, constitute what has been labeled the "National Labor Code": (1) the Wagner Act, (2) the Taft-Hartley Act, and (3) the Landrum-Griffin Act. Each act was passed to focus on some facet of the relationships between unions and management.

Wagner Act (National Labor Relations Act)

The National Labor Relations Act, more commonly referred to as the Wagner Act, has been called the Magna Carta of labor and is, by anyone's standards, pro-union. Passed in 1935, the Wagner Act was an outgrowth of the Great Depression.

With employers having to close or cut back their operations, workers were left with little job security. Unions stepped in to provide a feeling of solidarity and strength for many workers. The Wagner Act declared, in effect, that the official policy of the U.S. government was to encourage collective bargaining.

The Wagner Act established the principle that employees would be protected in their right to form a union and to bargain collectively. To protect union rights, the act prohibited employers from undertaking the following five unfair labor practices:

▶ Interfering with, restraining, or coercing employees in the exercise of their right to organize or to bargain collectively.
▶ Dominating or interfering with the formation or administration of any labor organization.
▶ Encouraging or discouraging membership in any labor organization by discriminating with regard to hiring, tenure, or conditions of employment.
▶ Discharging or otherwise discriminating against an employee because he or she filed charges or gave testimony under the act.
▶ Refusing to bargain collectively with representatives of the employees.

The National Labor Relations Board (NLRB) administers all provisions of the Wagner Act and subsequent labor relations acts. Although it was set up as an impartial umpire of the organizing process, the NLRB has altered its emphasis depending on which political party is in power to appoint members.[2]

Taft-Hartley Act (Labor-Management Relations Act)

The passage in 1947 of the Labor-Management Relations Act, better known as the Taft-Hartley Act, answered the concerns of many who felt that unions had become too strong. An attempt to balance the collective bargaining equation, this act was designed to offset the pro-union Wagner Act by limiting union actions; therefore, it was considered to be pro-management. It became the second part of the National Labor Code.

The new law amended or qualified in some respect all of the major provisions of the Wagner Act and established an entirely new code of conduct for unions. The Taft-Hartley Act forbade unions from a series of unfair labor practices that were very much like those prohibited for management. Coercion, discrimination against nonmembers, refusing to bargain, excessive membership fees, and other practices were forbidden for unions. The Taft-Hartley Act also allows the president of the United States to declare that a strike presents a national emergency. A **national emergency strike** is one that would affect an industry or a major part of it such that the national economy would be significantly affected.

One specific provision of the Taft-Hartley Act, Section 14(b), deserves special explanation. This "right-to-work" provision affects the **closed shop**, which requires individuals to join a union before they can be hired. Because of concerns that a closed shop allows a union to "control" who may be considered for employment and who must be hired by an employer, Section 14(b) prohibits the closed shop except in construction-related occupations.

Landrum-Griffin Act (Labor-Management Reporting and Disclosure Act)

In 1959 the third segment of the National Labor Code, the Landrum-Griffin Act, was passed. A congressional committee investigating the Teamsters union had found corruption in the union. The law was aimed at protecting the rights of individual union members against such practices. Under the Landrum-Griffin Act, unions must have bylaws, financial reports must be made, union members must have a bill of rights, and the Secretary of Labor will act as a watchdog of union conduct. Because a union is supposed to be a democratic institution in which union members vote on and elect officers and approve labor contracts, the Landrum-Griffin Act was passed in part to ensure that the federal government protects those democratic rights.

In a few instances, union officers have attempted to maintain their jobs by physically harassing or attacking individuals who try to oust them from office. In other cases, union officials have "milked" pension fund monies for their own use. Such instances are not typical of most unions, but illustrate the need for legislative oversight to protect individual union members.

Labor organizations have developed complex organizational structures with multiple levels. The broadest level is the **federation**, which is a group of autonomous national and international unions. **National unions** and **international unions** are not governed by the federation even if they are affiliated with it. They collect dues and have their own boards, specialized publications, and separate constitutions and bylaws. Such national-international unions as the United Steel Workers and the American Federation of State, County, and Municipal Employees determine broad union policy and offer services to local union units. **Local unions** may be centered on a particular employer organization or around a particular geographic location. Officers in local unions are elected by the membership and are subject to removal if they do not perform satisfactorily. For this reason, local union officers tend to be concerned with how they are perceived by the union members. They tend to react to situations as politicians do because they, too, are concerned about obtaining votes.

THE PROCESS OF UNIONIZING

The process of unionizing an employer may begin in one of two primary ways: (1) union targeting of an industry or company, or (2) based on employees' requests. In the former case, the local or national union identifies a firm or industry in which it believes unionization can succeed. The logic for targeting is that if the union is successful in one firm or a portion of the industry, then many other workers in the industry will be more willing to consider unionizing.

The second impetus for union organizing occurs when individual workers in an organization contact a union and express a desire to unionize. The employees themselves—or the union—then may begin to campaign to win support among the other employees.

Once the unionizing efforts begin, all activities must conform to the requirements established by labor laws and the National Labor Relations Board for private-sector employees, or by the appropriate federal or state governmental agency for public-sector employees. Both management and the unions must adhere to those requirements, or the results of the effort can be appealed to the NLRB and overturned.

Like other entities seeking members, a union usually mounts an organized campaign to persuade individuals to support its efforts. This persuasion takes many forms, including personally contacting employees outside work, mailing materials to employees' homes, inviting employees to attend special meetings away from the company, and publicizing the advantages of union membership.

A **union authorization card** is signed by an employee to designate a union as his or her collective bargaining agent. At least 30% of the employees in the targeted group must sign authorization cards before an election can be called. If two unions are attempting to represent employees, the employees will have three choices: union A, union B, or no union. Before the election is held, the appropriate bargaining unit must be determined. A **bargaining unit** is composed of all employees eligible to select a single union to represent and bargain collectively for them. If management and the union do not agree on who is and who is not included in the unit, the regional office of the NLRB must make a determination.

Employers and unions engage in a number of activities before an election. Both the Wagner Act and the Taft-Hartley Act place restrictions on these activities. Figure 11-3 lists some common tactics that management legally can use and some tactics it cannot use.

Various tactics may be used by management representatives in attempting to defeat a unionization effort. Such tactics often begin when handbills appear, or when authorization cards are being distributed. Some employers hire experts who specialize in combating unionization efforts. Using these "union busters," as they are called by unions, appears to enhance employers' chances of winning the representation election.

Assuming an election is held, the union need receive only the votes of a majority of those voting in the election. For example, if a group of two-hundred employees is the identified unit, and only fifty people vote, only 50% of the employees voting plus one (in this case, twenty-six) would need to vote yes in order for the union to be named as the representative of all two-hundred employees.

Employees who have a union and no longer wish to be represented by it can use the election process called **decertification**. The decertification process is similar to the unionization process. Employees attempting to oust a union must obtain decertification authorization cards signed by at least 30% of the employees in the bargaining unit before an election may be called. If a majority of those

FIGURE 11-3   Legal Do's and Don'ts for Managers during the Unionization Process

DO (LEGAL)	DON'T (ILLEGAL)
• Tell employees about current wages and benefits and how they compare with those in other firms • Tell employees that the employer opposes unionization • Tell employees the disadvantages of having a union (especially cost of dues, assessments, and requirements of membership) • Show employees articles about unions and relate negative experiences others have had elsewhere • Explain the unionization process to employees accurately • Forbid distribution of union literature during work hours in work areas • Enforce disciplinary policies and rules consistently and appropriately	• Promise employees pay increases or promotions if they vote against the union • Threaten employees with termination or discriminate when disciplining employees • Threaten to close down or move the company if a union is voted in • Spy on or have someone spy on union meetings • Make a speech to employees or groups at work within 24 hours of the election (before that, it is allowed) • Ask employees how they plan to vote or if they have signed authorization cards • Encourage employees to persuade others to vote against the union (such a vote must be initiated solely by the employee)

voting in the election want to remove the union, the decertification effort succeeds. Newly certified unions are given at least a year before decertification can be attempted by workers in the bargaining unit.[3]

Collective bargaining, the last step in unionization, is the process whereby representatives of management and workers negotiate over wages, hours, and other terms and conditions of employment. It is a give-and-take process between representatives of two organizations for the benefit of both. It is also a relationship based on relative power. The power relationship in collective bargaining involves conflict, and the threat of conflict seems necessary to maintain the relationship. But perhaps the most significant aspect of collective bargaining is that it is a continuing relationship that does not end immediately after agreement is reached. Instead, it continues for the life of the labor agreement and beyond.

Virtually all labor contracts include **management rights provisions**, which are those rights reserved to the employer to manage, direct, and control its business. Such a provision often reads as follows:

The employer retains all rights to manage, direct, and control its business in all particulars, except as such rights are expressly and specifically modified by the terms of this or any subsequent agreement.

By including such a provision, management is attempting to preserve its unilateral right to decide to make changes in any areas not identified in a labor contract.

A major concern of union representatives when bargaining is to negotiate **union security provisions**, which are contract provisions to aid the union in obtaining and retaining members. One union security provision is the **dues checkoff**, which provides that union dues will be deducted automatically from the payroll checks of union members. This provision makes it much easier for the union to collect its funds, which it must otherwise collect by billing each member separately.

A growing facet of union security in labor contracts is the *no-layoff policy,* or *job security guarantee.* This is especially true in light of all of the mergers, downsizings, and job reductions taking place in many industries.

Collective Bargaining

Both labor and management representatives spend much time preparing for negotiations. Employer and industry data concerning wages, benefits, working conditions, management and union rights, productivity, and absenteeism are gathered. If the organization argues that it cannot afford to pay what the union is asking, the employer's financial situation and accompanying data are all the more relevant. However, the union must request such information before the employer is obligated to provide it.

Typical bargaining includes initial proposals of expectations by both sides. The amount of rancor or calmness exhibited sets the tone for future negotiations between the parties. After opening positions have been taken, each side attempts to determine what the other values highly so the best bargain can be struck. For example, the union may be asking the employer to pay for dental benefits as part of a package that also includes wage demands and retirement benefits. However, the union may be most interested in the wages and retirement benefits.

Provisions in federal law require that both employer and employee bargaining representatives negotiate in *good faith.* In good-faith negotiations, the parties agree to send negotiators who can bargain and make decisions, rather than people who do not have the authority to commit either group to a decision.

After an initial agreement has been made, the bargaining parties usually return to their respective constituencies to determine whether or not what they have informally agreed on is acceptable. A particularly crucial stage is **ratification** of the labor agreement, which occurs when union members vote to accept the terms of a negotiated agreement.

Bargaining Impasse

Regardless of the structure of the bargaining process, labor and management do not always reach agreement on the issues. If impasse occurs, then the disputes can be taken to conciliation, mediation, or arbitration.

Conciliation and Mediation. When an impasse occurs, an outside party may aid the two deadlocked parties to continue negotiations and arrive at a solution. In **conciliation**, the third party attempts to keep union and management negotiators talking so that they can reach a voluntary settlement but makes no proposals for solutions. In **mediation**, the third party assists the negotiators in their discussions and also suggests settlement proposals. In neither conciliation nor mediation does the third party attempt to impose a solution.

Arbitration. The process of **arbitration** is a process that uses a neutral third party to make a decision. It can be conducted by either an individual or a panel of individuals. Arbitration is used to solve bargaining impasses primarily in the public sector. This "interest" arbitration is not frequently used in the private sector, because companies generally do not want an outside party making decisions about their rights, wages, benefits, and other issues. However, grievance or "rights" arbitration is used extensively in the private sector.

Strikes and Lockouts

If a deadlock cannot be resolved, then an employer may revert to a lockout—or a union may revert to a strike. During a **strike**, union members refuse to work in order to put pressure on an employer. Often, striking union members picket or demonstrate against the employer outside the place of business by carrying placards and signs. In a **lockout**, management shuts down company operations to prevent union members from working. This action may avert possible damage or sabotage to company facilities or injury to employees who continue to work. It also provides leverage to managers.

The following types of strikes can occur:

- ▶ *Economic strikes* occur when the parties fail to reach agreement during collective bargaining.
- ▶ *Unfair labor practice strikes* occur when union members walk away from their jobs over what they feel are illegal employer actions, such as the refusal to bargain.
- ▶ *Wildcat strikes* occur during the life of the collective bargaining agreement without approval of union leadership and violate a no-strike clause in a labor contract. Strikers can be discharged or disciplined.
- ▶ *Jurisdictional strikes* occur when one union's members walk out to force the employer to assign work to them instead of to another union.

▶ *Sympathy strikes* express one union's support for another union involved in a dispute, even though the first union has no disagreement with the employer.

Workers' rights vary depending on the type of strike that occurs.[4] For example, in an economic strike, an employer is free to replace the striking workers. But with an unfair labor practices strike, workers who want their jobs back at the end of the strike must be reinstated.

MANAGEMENT'S CHOICE: COOPERATE OR STAY NONUNION

The adversarial relationship that naturally exists between unions and management may lead to conflicts. But there is also a greater recognition by many union leaders and employer representatives that cooperation between management and labor unions is sensible if organizations are going to compete in a global economy. An alternative to management cooperating with a union is to try to stay nonunion. The choice between the two is a strategic HR decision that each employer must make.

Cooperation and Employee Involvement

Companies often cited as examples of successful union-management cooperation include National Steel Corporation, Scott Paper Company, Saturn, and Xerox. All have established cooperative programs of one sort or another that include employee involvement. Some in the labor movement fear that such programs may lead to an undermining of union support by creating a closer identification with the company's concerns and goals.

Unions have become active participants by encouraging workers to become partial or complete owners of the companies that employ them. These efforts were spurred by concerns that firms were preparing to shut down, or to be merged or bought out by financial investors who the unions feared would cut union jobs. Unions have assisted members in putting together employee stock ownership plans (ESOPs) to purchase all or part of some firms.

Staying Nonunion

Employees may make a strategic decision to remain nonunion. Such a choice is perfectly rational, but may require some different HR policies and philosophies to accomplish. *Preventative employee relations* may emphasize good morale and loyalty based on concern for employees, competitive wages and benefits, a good system for dealing with employee complaints, and safe working conditions. Other issues may also play a part in employees' decisions to stay nonunion, but if the points listed here are adequately addressed, few workers will feel the need for a union to represent them to management.[5]

GRIEVANCE MANAGEMENT

Unions know that employee dissatisfaction is a potential source of trouble, whether it is expressed or not. Hidden dissatisfaction grows and creates reactions that may be completely out of proportion to the original concerns. Therefore, it is important that dissatisfaction be given an outlet. A **complaint**, which is merely an indication of employee dissatisfaction that has not been submitted in writing, is one outlet.

If the employee is represented by a union, and the employee says, "I should have received the job transfer because I have more seniority, which is what the union contract states," and she submits it in writing, then that complaint is a grievance. A **grievance** is a complaint that has been put in writing and thus made formal. Management should be concerned with both complaints and grievances, because both may be important indicators of potential problems within the workforce. Without a grievance procedure, management may be unable to respond to employee concerns because managers are unaware of them. Therefore, a formal grievance procedure is a valuable communication tool for the organization.[6]

Grievance procedures are formal communications channels designed to settle a grievance as soon as possible after the problem arises. First-line supervisors are usually closest to a problem; however, the supervisor is concerned with many other matters besides one employee's grievance, and may even be the subject of an employee's grievance. A unionized employee generally has a right to union representation if he or she is being questioned by management and if discipline may result. If these so-called *Weingarten rights* (named after the court case that established them) are violated and the employee is dismissed, he or she usually will be reinstated with back pay.

Steps in a Grievance Procedure

Grievance procedures can vary in the number of steps they include. Some or all of the following steps may occur:

1. The employee discusses the grievance with the union steward (the union's representative on the job) and the supervisor.
2. The union steward discusses the grievance with the supervisor's manager.
3. The union grievance committee discusses the grievance with appropriate company managers.
4. The representative of the national union discusses the grievance with designated company executives.
5. The final step may be to use an impartial third party for ultimate disposition of the grievance.

If the grievance remains unsettled, representatives for both sides would continue to meet to resolve the conflict. On rare occasions, a representative from the national union might join the process. Or, a corporate executive from headquarters (if the firm is a large corporation) might be called in to help resolve the grievance. If not solved at this stage, the grievance goes to arbitration.

Arbitration is flexible and can be applied to almost any kind of controversy except those involving criminal matters. Advisory, or voluntary, arbitration may be used in negotiating agreements or in interpreting clauses in existing agreements. Because labor and management generally agree that disputes over the negotiation of a new contract should not be arbitrated in the private sector, the most important role played by arbitration in labor relations is as the final step in the grievance procedure.[7]

Grievance arbitration is a means by which disputes arising from different interpretations of a labor contract are settled by a third party. This should not be confused with contract or issues arbitration, discussed earlier, when arbitration is used to determine how a contract will be written.

Grievance arbitration presents several problems. It has been criticized as being too costly, too legalistic, and too time-consuming. In addition, many feel that there are too few qualified and experienced arbitrators. Despite these problems, arbitration has been successful and is currently seen as a potentially superior solution to traditional approaches to resolving union-management problems.

NOTES

1. William P. Webster, "Maintaining Quality Relationships between Labor and Management," *National Productivity Review,* Spring 1997, 63–69.
2. James Worsham, "A Course Change at the NLRB," *Nation's Business,* February 1998, 36.
3. Robert W. Schupp, "When Is a Union Not a Union?" *Labor Law Journal* 48, 1997, 359–370.
4. T. Zane Reeves, "Strikes—Are They Useful Anymore?" *Journal of Collective Negotia-* *tions in the Public Sector,* Winter 1997, 65–71.
5. Jackson Lewis, *Winning NLRB Elections* (Chicago: CCH Inc., 1997).
6. Robert P. Hebdon and Robert N. Hebdon, "Tradeoffs among Expressions of Industrial Conflict," *Industrial and Labor Relations Review,* 50, 1998, 204–221.
7. Kay O. Wilburn, "Employee Disputes: Solving Them out of Court," *Management Review,* March 1998, 17–21.

SUGGESTED READINGS

T.O. Collier, *Supervisor's Guide to Labor Relations,* SHRM, 1998.

John A. Fossum, *Labor Relations,* 7th ed., BPI-Irwin, 1999.

Court D. Gifford, *Directory of U.S. Organizations,* Bureau of National Affairs, 2000.

Wendy Trach-Huber and Stephen K. Huber, *Mediation and Negotiation,* Anderson Publishing, 1998.

SUGGESTED INTERNET RESOURCES

AFL-CIO. Contains union-related information.
http://www.afl-cio.org

National Labor Relations Board. Provides information on this U.S. government agency, which enforces and administers labor-management laws and regulations.
http://www.nlrb.gov

Appendix A
Content Outline of the HR Body of Knowledge©

After each of the major functional sub-areas are the weightings for that sub-area. **The first number in the parentheses is the PHR percentage weighting and the second number is the SPHR percentage weighting.** These weightings should help you allocate your time in preparing for each respective examination.

I. Management Practices (15%, 21%)
   A. Role of HR in Organizations (2.78%, 3.91%)
     1. HR Roles: Advisory Counselor, Consultant, Service, Control
     2. Change Agent Role/Reengineering and Facilitating Both Content & Process
     3. HR's Role in Strategic Planning
     4. HR Generalist and HR Specialist Roles
     5. Effects of Different Organizational Contexts and Industries on HR functions
     6. HR Policies and Procedures
     7. Integration and Coordination of HR Functions
     8. Outsourcing the HR Functions
   B. Human Resource Planning (2.04%, 2.87%)
     1. Environmental Scanning
     2. Internal Scanning
     3. Human Resources Inventory
     4. Human Resource Information Systems
     5. Action Plans and Programs
     6. Evaluation of Human Resource Planning
   C. Organizational Design and Development (.65%, .99%)
     1. Organizational Structures
     2. Organizational Development

---

      3. Diagnosis and Intervention Strategies: Action Research, Sensing, Team Building, Goal Setting, Survey Feedback, Strategic Planning, Visioning, Sensitivity Training (T-groups), Grid Training

      4. Role of Organizational Culture in Organizational Development

      5. Role of International Culture in Organizational Development

      6. Organizational Development in Response to Technological Change

  D. Budgeting, Controlling, and Measurement (1.08%, 1.56%)

      1. HR Budgeting Process

      2. HR Control Process

      3. Evaluating HR Effectiveness

  E. Motivation (.59%, .77%)

      1. Motivation Theories

      2. Applying Motivation Theory in Management

  F. Leadership (.97%, 1.32%)

      1. Leadership Theories

      2. Effect of Leadership in Organizations

      3. Leadership training

  G. Quality and Performance Management/TQM (1.82%, 2.41%)

      1. Performance Planning: Identifying Goals/Desired Behaviors

      2. Setting and Communicating Performance Standards

      3. Measuring Results and Providing Feedback

      4. Implementing Performance Improvement Strategies

      5. Evaluating Results

  H. Employee Involvement Strategies (2.11%, 2.57%)

      1. Work Teams

      2. Job Design and Redesign

      3. Employee Ownership/ESOPs

      4. Employee Suggestion System

      5. Participative Management

      6. Alternative Work Schedules

      7. Role of HR in Employee Involvement Programs

  I. HR Research (.71%, 1.16%)

      1. Research Design and Methodology

      2. Quantitative Analysis

      3. Qualitative Research

  J. International HR Management (1.49%, 2.48%)

      1. Cultural Differences

      2. Legal Aspects of International HR

      3. Expatriation and Repatriation

      4. Issues of Multinational Corporations

      5. Compensation and Benefits for Foreign Nationals and Expatriates

      6. The Role of HR in International Business

  K. Ethics (.77%, .96%)

      1. Ethical Issues

      2. Establishing Ethical Behavior in the Organization

II. General Employment Practices (19%, 17%)

   A. Legal & Regulatory Factors: Definitions, Requirements, Proscribed Practices, Exemptions, Enforcement, Remedies, & Case Histories (6.38%, 5.29%)

     1. Title VII of the Civil Rights Act (1964) as Amended (1972, 1991)

     2. Age Discrimination in Employment Act (1967) as Amended

     3. Health, Medical, & Rehabilitation Statutes (e.g., Vocational Rehabilitation Act, Pregnancy Discrimination Act, Americans with Disabilities Act, Family & Medical Leave Act, HMO Act, etc.)

     4. Vietnam-Era Veterans Readjustment act (1986)

     5. Immigration Reform and Control Act (1986) as Amended (1990)

     6. Employee Polygraph Protection Act (1988)

     7. Uniform Guidelines on Employee Selection Procedures

     8. Worker Adjustment and Retraining Notification Act (1988)

     9. North American Free Trade Act

     10. Common Law Tort Theories

     11. Copyright Statutes

     12. Compensation Laws and Regulations

     13. Consumer Credit Protection Act: Wage Garnishment (1968), Fair Credit Reporting (1970)

     14. Social Security/Retirement Legislation (e.g., ERISA)

     15. COBRA (Consolidated Omnibus Budget Reconciliation Act (1990)); Omnibus Budget Reconciliation Act (1993)

     16. Workers' Compensation and Unemployment Compensation Laws and Regulations

     17. Legal and Regulatory Factors Affecting Employee and Labor Relations (e.g., NLRA, Taft-Hartley, Landrum-Griffin, etc.)

     18. Federal Health, Safety, and Security Legislation (e.g., OSHA)

   B. Job Analysis, Job Description, and Job Specification (2.14%, 1.78%)

     1. Methods of Job Analysis

     2. Types of Data Gathered in a Job Analysis

     3. Uses of Job Analysis

     4. Job Descriptions

     5. Job/Position Specifications

     6. Validity & Reliability of Job Analysis, Job Description, & Job Specification

   C. Individual Employment Rights (1.72%, 1.67%)

     1. Employment-at-Will Doctrine

     2. Exceptions to Employment-at-Will

     3. Common Law Tort Theories

     4. Job-as-Property Doctrine

     5. Non-Compete Agreement

   D. Performance Appraisals (5.10%, 4.60%)

     1. Performance Measurement—The Criterion

     2. Criterion Problems

    3. Documenting Employee Performance
    4. Category Rating Appraisal Methods
    5. Comparative Appraisal Methods
    6. Narrative Appraisal Methods
    7. Special Appraisal Methods: MBO, BARS, BOS
    8. Types of Appraisals
    9. Rating Errors
    10. Appraisal Interview
    11. Linking Appraisals to Employment Decisions
    12. Legal Constraints on Performance Appraisal
    13. Documentation

E. Workplace Behavior Problems (1.90%, 1.55%)
    1. Discipline
    2. Absenteeism and Tardiness
    3. Sexual Harassment
    4. Drug and Alcohol Use
    5. Off-Duty Conduct

F. Employee Attitudes, Opinions, and Satisfaction (2.01%, 2.11%)
    1. Measurement
    2. Results Analysis
    3. Interpretation
    4. Feedback
    5. Intervention
    6. Confidentiality and Anonymity of Surveys

III. Staffing (19%, 15%)

A. Equal Employment Opportunity/Affirmative Action (3.56%, 2.99%)
    1. Legal Endorsement of EEO: Supreme Court Decisions
    2. Equal Employment Opportunity Programs
    3. Affirmative Action Plans
    4. Special Programs to Eliminate Discrimination
    5. Fairness Issues: Reverse Discrimination, Quota Hiring vs. Merit Hiring

B. Recruitment (2.84%, 2.22%)
    1. Determining Recruitment Needs and Objectives
    2. Identifying Selection Criteria
    3. Internal Sourcing
    4. External Sourcing
    5. Evaluating Recruiting Effectiveness

C. Selection (5.94%, 4.39%)
    1. Application Process
    2. Interviewing
    3. Pre-Employment Testing
    4. Background Investigation
    5. Medical Examination
    6. Hiring Applicants with Disabilities

       7. Illegal Use of Drugs and Alcohol
       8. Validation and Evaluation of Selection Process Components
   D. Career Planning and Development (2.06%, 1.84%)
       1. Accommodating Organizational and Individual Needs
       2. Mobility within the Organization
       3. Managing Transitions
   E. Organizational Exit (4.60%, 3.56%)
       1. General Issues
       2. Layoffs/Reductions-in-Force
       3. Constructive Discharge
       4. Retaliatory
       5. Retirement
       6. Employer Defenses against Litigation

IV. Human Resource Development (11%, 12%)
   A. HR Training and the Organization (3.06%, 3.72%)
       1. The Learning Organization, Linking Training to Organizational
          Goals, Objectives, and Strategies
       2. Human Resources Development as an Organizational Component
       3. Funding the Training Function
       4. Cost/Benefit Analysis of Training
   B. Training Needs Analysis (1.52%, 1.52%)
       1. Training Needs Analysis Process
       2. Methods for Assessing Training Needs
   C. Training and Development Programs (4.42%, 4.50%)
       1. Trainer Selection
       2. Design Considerations and Learning Principles
       3. Types of Training Programs
       4. Instructional Methods and Processes
       5. Training Facilities Planning
       6. Training Materials
   D. Evaluation of Training Effectiveness (2.00%, 2.26%)
       1. Sources for Evaluation
       2. Research Methods for Evaluation
       3. Criteria for Evaluating Training

V. Compensation and Benefits (19%, 15%)
   A. Tax & Accounting Treatment of Compensation & Benefit Programs
      (.57%, .53%)
       1. FASB Regulations
       2. IRS Regulations
   B. Economic Factors Affecting Compensation (2.09%, 1.77%)
       1. Inflation
       2. Interest Rates
       3. Industry Competition
       4. Foreign Competition

  5. Economic Growth
  6. Labor Market Trends/Demographics
C. Compensation Philosophy, Strategy, and Policy (1.81%, 1.55%)
  1. Fitting Strategy & Policy to the External Environment and to an
      Organization's Culture, Structure, & Objectives
  2. Training in and Communication of Compensation Programs
  3. Making Compensation Programs Achieve Organizational Objects
  4. Establishing Administrative Controls
D. Compensation Programs: Types, Characteristics, and Advantages/
    Disadvantages (1.71%, 1.20%)
  1. Base Pay
  2. Differential Pay
  3. Incentive Pay
  4. Pay Programs for Selected Employees
E. Job Evaluation Methods (2.20%, 1.60%)
  1. Compensable Factors
  2. Ranking Method
  3. Classification/Grading Method
  4. Factor Comparison Method
  5. Point Method
  6. Guide Chart-Profile Method (Hay Method)
F. Job Pricing, Pay Structures, and Pay Rate Administration (2.14%,
    1.49%)
  1. Job Pricing and Pay Structures
  2. Individual Pay Rate Determination
  3. Utilizing Performance Appraisal in Pay Administration
  4. Reflecting Market Influences in Pay Structures
  5. Wage Surveys
G. Employee Benefit Programs: Types, Objectives, Characteristics, and
    Advantages/Disadvantages (3.42%, 2.17%)
  1. Legally Required Programs/Payments
  2. Income Replacement
  3. Insurance and Income Protection
  4. Deferred Pay
  5. Pay for Time Not Worked
  6. Unpaid Leave
  7. Flexible Benefit Plans
  8. Recognition and Achievement Awards
H. Managing Employee Benefit Programs (3.75%, 3.43%)
  1. Employee Benefits Philosophy, Planning, and Strategy
  2. Employee Need/Preference Assessment: Surveys
  3. Administrative Systems
  4. Funding/Investment Responsibilities
  5. Coordination with Plan Trustees, Insurers, Health Service Providers,
      and Third-Party Administrators

6. Utilization Review
7. Cost-Benefit Analysis and Cost Management
8. Communicating Benefit Programs/Individual Annual Benefits Reports
9. Monitoring Compensation/Benefits Legal Compliance Programs

I. Evaluating Total Compensation Strategy & Program Effectiveness (1.32%, 1.26%)
   1. Budgeting
   2. Cost Management
   3. Assessment of Methods and Processes

VI. Employee and Labor Relations (11%, 14%)
   A. Union Representation of Employees (1.52%, 1.98%)
      1. Scope of the Labor Management Relations (Taft-Hartley) Act (1947)
      2. Achieving Representative Status
      3. Petitioning for an NLRB Election
      4. Election Campaign
      5. Union security
   B. Employer Unfair Labor Practices (1.68%, 1.91%)
      1. Procedures for Processing Charges of Unfair Labor Practices
      2. Interference, Restraint, and Coercion
      3. Domination and Unlawful Support of Labor Organization
      4. Employee Discrimination to Discourage Union Membership
      5. Retaliation
      6. Remedies
   C. Union Unfair Labor Practices, Strikes, and Boycotts (1.96%, 2.60%)
      1. Responsibility for Acts of Union Agents
      2. Union Restraint or Coercion
      3. Duty of Fair Representation
      4. Inducing Unlawful Discrimination by Employer
      5. Excessive or Discriminatory Membership Fees
      6. Strikes and Secondary Boycotts
      7. Strike Preparation
   D. Collective Bargaining (2.94%, 4.06%)
      1. Bargaining Issues and Concepts
      2. Negotiation Strategies
      3. Good Faith Requirements
      4. Notice Requirements
      5. Unilateral Changes in Terms of Employment
      6. Duty to Successor Employers or Unions: Buyouts, Mergers, or Bankruptcy
      7. Enforcement Provisions
      8. Injunctions
      9. Mediation and Conciliation
     10. National Emergency Strikes

E. Managing Organization-Union Relations (.88%, 1.16%)
   1. Building and Maintaining Union-Organization Relationships: Cooperative Programs
   2. Grievance Processes and Procedures
   3. Dispute Resolution
F. Maintaining Nonunion Status (.79%, .91%)
   1. Reasons
   2. Strategies
G. Public Sector Labor Relations (1.12%, 1.38%)
   1. Right to Organize
   2. Federal Labor Relations Council
   3. Limitations on Strikes
   4. Mediation and Conciliation

VII. Health, Safety, and Security (6%, 6%)
   A. Health (2.41%, 2.22%)
      1. Employee Assistance Programs
      2. Employee Wellness Programs
      3. Reproductive Health Policies
      4. Chemical Dependency
      5. Communicable Diseases in the Workplace
      6. Employer Liabilities
      7. Stress Management
      8. Smoking Policies
      9. Recordkeeping and Reporting
   B. Safety (2.05%, 2.04%)
      1. Areas of Concern
      2. Organization of Safety Program
      3. Safety Promotion
      4. Accident Investigation
      5. Safety Inspections
      6. Human Factors Engineering (Ergonomics)
      7. Special Safety Considerations
      8. Sources of Assistance
   C. Security (1.54%, 1.74%)
      1. Organization of Security
      2. Control Systems
      3. Protection of Proprietary Information
      4. Crisis Management and Contingency Planning
      5. Theft and Fraud
      6. Investigations and Preventive Corrections

Appendix B
Important Organizations in HR Management

ASSOCIATIONS

Academy of Management
P.O. Box 3020
Briarcliff Manor, NY   10510-3020
http://www.aom.pace.edu

AFL-CIO
815 - 16th Street, NW
Washington, DC   20006
http://www.afl-cio.org

American Arbitration Association
140 W. 51st Street
New York, NY   10020
http://www.adr.org

American Management Association
1601 Broadway
New York, NY   10019-7420
http://www.amanet.org

American Payroll Association
30 East 33rd Street, 5th Floor
New York, NY   10016-5386
http://www.americanpayroll.org

American Society for Industrial Security
1624 Prince Street
Arlington, VA   22314
http://www.asisonline.org

American Society for Public Administration
1120 G Street, NW, Suite 700
Washington, DC   20005
http://www.aspanet.org

American Society for Training and Development
1640 King Street
P.O. Box 1443
Alexandria, VA 22313-2043
http://www.astd.org

American Society of Safety Engineers
1800 East Oakton
Des Plaines, IL 60018
http://www.asse.org

American Staffing Association
119 South Saint Asaph Street
Alexandria, VA 22314-3119
http://www.natss.org

Association of Executive Search Consultants
500 Fifth Avenue, Suite 930
New York, NY 10110
http://www.aesc.org

Chartered Institute of Personnel and Development
CIPD House
Camp Road, Wimbledon
London SW19 4UX
England
http://www.ipd.co.uk

College and University Professional Association for Human Resources
1233 20th Street, NW, Suite 301
Washington, DC   20036
http://www.cupahr.org

The Conference Board
845 Third Avenue
New York, NY 10022-6679
http://www.conference-board.org

Employee Benefit Research Institute
2121 K Street, NW, Suite 600
Washington, DC 20037-1896
http://www.ebri.org

Employee Relocation Council
1720 N Street, NW
Washington, DC 20036-2900
http://www.erc.org

Employee Services Management Association
2211 York Road, Suite 207
Oak Brook, IL 60523
http://www.esmassn.org

ESOP Association
1726 M Street, NW, Suite 501
Washington, DC 20036
http://www.the-esop-emplowner.org

Human Resource Certification Institute (HRCI)
1800 Duke Street
Alexandria, VA 22314
http://www.shrm.org/hrci

Human Resource Planning Society
317 Madison Avenue, Suite 1509
New York, NY 10017
http://www.hrps.org

Incentive Manufacturers Representatives Association
1805 North Mill Street, Suite A
Naperville, IL 60563-1275
http://www.imra1.org

Industrial Relations Research Association
4233 Social Science Building
University of Wisconsin-Madison
1180 Observatory Drive
Madison, WI 53706-1373
http://www.irra.uiuc.edu

International Association for Human Resource Information Management
401 North Michigan Avenue
Chicago, IL 60611
http://www.ihrim.org

International Foundation of Employee Benefit Plans
18700 Bluemound Road
Brookfield, WI 53008-0069
http://www.ifebp.org

International Personnel Management Association
1617 Duke Street
Alexandria, VA 22314
http://www.ipma-hr.org

National Association for the Advancement of Colored People (NAACP)
4805 Mt. Hope Drive
Baltimore, MD 21215
http://www.naacp.org

National Association of Manufacturers (NAM)
1331 Pennsylvania Avenue, NW
Washington, DC 20004-1790
http://www.nam.org

Society for Human Resource Management (SHRM)
1800 Duke Street
Alexandria, VA 22314
http://www.shrm.org

U.S. Chamber of Commerce
1615 H Street, NW
Washington, DC 20062
http://www.uschamber.org

Wellness Councils of America
Community Health Plaza, Suite 311
7101 Newport Avenue
Omaha, NE 68152
http://www.welcoa.org

World at Work
14040 N. Northsight Blvd.
Scottsdale, AZ   85260
http://www.worldatwork.org

U.S. DEPARTMENT OF LABOR AGENCIES

The following agencies are part of and have the same address as the Department of Labor:

U.S. Department of Labor
200 Constitution Avenue, NW
Washington, DC 20210
http://www.dol.gov

Bureau of Labor Statistics
http://www.bls.gov

Wage and Hour Division
Employment Standards Administration
http://www.dol.gov/dol/esa/public/whd-org.htm

Occupational Safety and Health Administration (OSHA)
http://www.osha.gov

Office of Federal Contract Compliance Programs (OFCCP)
http://www.dol.gov/dol/esa/public/ofcp_org.htm

OTHER GOVERNMENT AGENCIES

Equal Employment Opportunity Commission (EEOC)
1801 L Street, NW
Washington, DC 20507
http://www.eeoc.gov

Federal Mediation and Conciliation Service
2100 K Street, NW
Washington, DC 20427
http://www.fmcs.gov

Office of Personnel Management
1900 E Street, NW
Washington, DC 20415-0001
http://www.opm.gov

Pension Benefit Guaranty Corporation
1200 K Street, NW
Washington, DC 2005-4026
http://www.pbgc.gov

Appendix C
Current Literature in HR Management

Students are expected to be familiar with the professional literature in their fields of study. The professional journals are the most immediate and direct communication link between the researcher and the practicing manager. Three groups of publications are listed in this appendix.

A. RESEARCH-ORIENTED JOURNALS

These journals contain articles that report on original research. Normally these journals contain either sophisticated writing and quantitative verifications of the author's findings or conceptual models and literature reviews of previous research.

Academy of Management Journal
Academy of Management Review
Administrative Science Quarterly
American Behavioral Scientist
American Journal of Health Promotion
American Journal of Psychology
American Journal of Sociology
American Psychological Measurement
American Psychologist
American Sociological Review
Annual Review of Psychology
Applied Psychology: An International Review
British Journal of Industrial Relations
Decision Sciences
Dispute Resolution Quarterly
Group and Organization Studies
Human Organization
Human Relations

Industrial & Labor Relations Review
Industrial Relations
Interfaces
Journal of Abnormal Psychology
Journal of Applied Behavioral Science
Journal of Applied Business Research
Journal of Applied Psychology
Journal of Business
Journal of Business Communications
Journal of Business and Industrial Marketing
Journal of Business and Psychology
Journal of Business Research
Journal of Communications
Journal of Compensation & Benefits
Journal of Counseling Psychology
Journal of Experimental Social Psychology
Journal of Human Resources
Journal of Industrial Relations
Journal of International Business Studies
Journal of Labor Economics
Journal of Management
Journal of Management Studies
Journal of Managerial Psychology
Journal of Occupational and Organizational Psychology
Journal of Organizational Behavior
Journal of Personality and Social Psychology
Journal of Quality Management
Journal of Quality & Participation
Journal of Social Issues
Journal of Social Policy
Journal of Social Psychology
Journal of Vocational Behavior
Labor History
Labor Relations Yearbook
Management Science
Organizational Behavior and Human Decision Processes
Personnel Psychology
Psychological Bulletin
Psychological Review
Social Forces
Social Science Research
Work and Occupations
World at Work Journal

B. MANAGEMENT-ORIENTED JOURNALS

These journals generally cover a wide range of subjects. Articles in these publications normally are aimed at the practitioner and are written to interpret, summarize, or discuss past, present, and future research and administrative applications. Not all the articles in these publications are management-oriented.

Academy of Management Executive
Administrative Management
Arbitration Journal
Australian Journal of Management
Benefits and Compensation Solutions
Business Horizons
Business Management
Business Monthly
Business Quarterly
Business and Social Review
California Management Review
Canadian Manager
Columbia Journal of World Business
Compensation and Benefits Management
Compensation and Benefits Review
Directors and Boards
Economist
Employee Benefits News
Employee Relations Law Journal
Employment Practices Decisions
Employment Relations
Employment Relations today
Entrepreneurship Theory and Practice
Forbes
Fortune
Harvard Business Review
Hospital & Health Services Administration
HR Magazine
Human Behavior
Human Resource Executive
Human Resource Management
Human Resource Planning
IHRIM Link
Inc.
Incentive
Industrial Management
Industry Week
International Management
Journal of Business Strategy

Journal of Pension Planning
Journal of Systems Management
Labor Law Journal
Long-Range Planning
Manage
Management Consulting
Management Review
Management Solutions
Management Today
Management World
Managers Magazine
Michigan State University Business Topics
Monthly Labor Review
Nation's Business
Occupational Health & Safety
Organizational Dynamics
Pension World
Personnel Management
Psychology Today
Public Administration Review
Public Manager
Public Opinion Quarterly
Public Personnel Management
Recruiting Today
Research Management
SAM Advanced Management Journal
Security Management
Sloan Management Review
Supervision
Supervisory Management
Training
Training and Development
Workforce
Working Woman
Workplace Ergonomics
World at Work News

C. ABSTRACTS & INDICES

For assistance in locating articles, students should check some of the following indices and abstracts that often contain subjects of interest.

ABI Inform
Applied Science and Technology Index
Applied Social Sciences Index and Abstracts

Business and Industry
Business and Management Practices
Business Periodicals
Compact Disclosure
Dissertation Abstracts
General BusinessFile ASAP
Human Resources Abstracts
Index to Legal Periodicals
Index to Social Sciences and Humanities
Investext
Legaltrac
Management Abstracts
Management Contents
Management Research Abstracts
Psychological Abstracts
Predicasts Prompt
PsychLit
PsycINFO
Reader's Guide to Periodical Literature
Sociological Abstracts
Wilson Business Abstracts
Work-Related Abstracts

Appendix D
Major Federal Equal Employment Opportunity Laws and Regulations

ACT	YEAR	PROVISIONS
Equal Pay Act	1963	Requires equal pay for men and women performing substantially the same work.
Title VII, Civil Rights Act of 1964	1964	Prohibits discrimination in employment on basis of race, color, religion, sex, or national origin
Executive Orders 11246 and 11375	1965 1967	Require federal contractors and subcontractors to eliminate employment discrimination and prior discrimination through affirmative action
Age Discrimination in Employment Act (as amended in 1978 and 1986)	1967	Prohibits discrimination against persons over age 40 and restricts mandatory retirement requirements, except where age is a bona-fide occupational qualification
Executive Order 11478	1969	Prohibits discrimination in the U.S. Postal Service and in the various government agencies on the basis of race, color, religion, sex, national origin, handicap, or age
Vocational Rehabilitation Act Rehabilitation Act of 1974	1973 1974	Prohibit employers with federal contracts over $2,500 from discriminating against individuals with disabilities
Vietnam-Era Veterans Readjustment Act	1974	Prohibits discrimination against Vietnam-era veterans by federal contractors and the U.S. government and requires affirmative action
Pregnancy Discrimination Act	1978	Prohibits discrimination against women affected by pregnancy, childbirth, or related medical conditions; requires that they be treated as all other employees for employment-related purposes, including benefits
Immigration Reform and Control Act	1986 1990 1996	Establishes penalties for employers who knowingly hire illegal aliens; prohibits employment discrimination on the basis of national origin or citizenship
Americans with Disabilities Act	1990	Requires employer accommodation of individuals with disabilities
Older Workers Benefit Protection Act of 1990	1990	Prohibits age-based discrimination in early retirement and other benefits plans
Civil Rights Act of 1991	1991	Overturns several past Supreme Court decisions and changes damage claims provisions
Congressional Accountability Act	1995	Extends EEO and Civil Rights Act provisions to U.S. congressional staff

Appendix E
Guidelines to Lawful and Unlawful
Preemployment Inquiries

SUBJECT OF INQUIRY	IT MAY NOT BE DISCRIMINATORY TO INQUIRE ABOUT:	IT MAY BE DISCRIMINATORY TO INQUIRE ABOUT:
1. Name	a. Whether applicant has ever worked under a different name	a. The original name of an applicant whose name has been legally changed b. The ethnic association of applicant's name
2. Age	a. If applicant is over the age of 18 b. If applicant is under the age of 18 or 21 if job related (i.e., selling liquor in retail store)	a. Date of birth b. Date of high school graduation
3. Residence	a. Applicant's place of residence; length of applicant's residence in state and/or city where employer is located	a. Previous addresses b. Birthplace of applicant or applicant's parents
4. Race of Color		a. Applicant's race or color of applicant's skin
5. National Origin and Ancestry		a. Applicant's lineage, ancestry, national origin, parentage, or nationality b. Nationality of applicant's parents or spouse
6. Sex and Family Composition		a. Sex of applicant b. Dependents of applicant c. Marital status d. Child-care arrangements
7. Creed or Religion		a. Applicant's religious affiliation b. Church, parish, or holidays observed
8. Citizenship	a. Whether the applicant is a citizen of the United States b. Whether the applicant is in the country on a visa that permits him or her to work or is a citizen	a. Whether applicant is a citizen of a country other than the United States

continues

Appendix E *Continued*

SUBJECT OF INQUIRY	IT MAY NOT BE DISCRIMINATORY TO INQUIRE ABOUT:	IT MAY BE DISCRIMINATORY TO INQUIRE ABOUT:
9. Language	a. Language applicant speaks and/or writes fluently, if job related	a. Applicant's native tongue; language commonly used at home
10. References	a. Names of persons willing to provide professional and/or character references for applicant	a. Name of applicant's pastor or religious leader
11. Relatives	a. Names of relatives already employed by the employer	a. Name and/or address of any relative of applicant b. Whom to contact in case of emergency
12. Organizations	a. Applicant's membership in any professional, service, or trade organization	a. All clubs or social organizations to which applicant belongs
13. Arrest Record and Convictions	a. Convictions, if related to job performance (disclaimer should accompany)	a. Number and kinds of arrests b. Convictions unless related to job performance
14. Photographs		a. Photograph with application, with résumé, or before hiring
15. Height and Weight		a. Any inquiry into height and weight of applicant except where a BFOQ
16. Physical Limitations	a. Whether applicant has the ability to perform job-related functions with or without accommodation	a. The nature or severity of an illness or the individuals's physical condition b. Whether applicant has ever filed a workers' compensation claim c. Any recent or past operations or surgery and dates
17. Education	a. Training applicant has received if related to the job under consideration b. Highest level of education attained, if validated that having certain educational background (e.g., high school diploma or college degree) is necessary to perform the specific job	
18. Military	a. What branch of the military applicant served in b. Type of education or training received in military c. Rank at discharge	a. Type of military discharge
19. Financial Status		a. Applicant's debts or assets b. Garnishments

Appendix F
Sample Job Description and Specifications

JOB TITLE: Compensation Administrator	**JOB CODE:** _____
INCUMBENT:	**GRADE:** _____
SUPERVISOR'S TITLE: Vice President of Human Resources	**FLSA STATUS:** Exempt_____
	EEOC CLASS: _O/M_____

General Summary: Responsible for the design and administration of all cash compensation programs, ensures proper consideration of the relationship of compensation to performance of each employee, and provides consultation on compensation administration to managers and supervisors.

Essential Duties and Responsibilities:

1. Prepares and maintains all job descriptions for all jobs and periodically reviews and updates all job descriptions. Responds to questions from employees and supervisors regarding job descriptions. (25%)

2. Ensures that Company compensation rates are in accordance with the Company philosophy. Maintains current information applicable to pay structure movements taking place in comparable organizations; obtains or conducts pay surveys as necessary and presents recommendations on pay structures on an annual basis. (20%)

3. Develops and administers the performance appraisal program and assists in the development of supervisory training programs. Monitors the use of the performance appraisal instruments to ensure the integrity of the system and its proper use. (20%)

4. Directs the job evaluation process by coordinating committee activities, and reevaluates jobs periodically through the committee process. Resolves disputes over proper evaluation of jobs. Conducts initial evaluation of new jobs prior to hiring and assigns jobs to pay ranges. (15%)

5. Researches and provides recommendations on executive compensation issues. Assists in the development and oversees the administration of all annual bonus payments for senior managers and executives. (15%)

6. Coordinates the development of an integrated Human Resource information system. Assists in identifying needs and interfaces with the Management Information Systems Department to achieve departmental goals for information needs. (5%)

7. Performs related duties as assigned or as the situation dictates.

continues

191

Appendix F *Continued*

Required Knowledge, Skills, and Abilities:

1. Knowledge of compensation and HR management practices and approaches.
2. Knowledge of effective job analysis methods and of survey development and interpretation practices and principles.
3. Knowledge of performance management program design and administration.
4. Knowledge of federal and state wage and hour regulations.
5. Skill in writing job descriptions, memorandums, letters, and proposals.
6. Skill in making presentations to groups and in explaining compensation policies and practices to employees and supervisors.
7. Ability to plan and prioritize work.
8. Ability to use spreadsheets, presentation graphics, word processing, and database computer software.

Education and Experience:

This position requires the equivalent of a college degree in Business Administration, Psychology, or a related field plus 3–5 years' experience in HR Management, 2–3 of which should include compensation administration experience. An advanced degree in Industrial Psychology, Business Administration, or HR Management is preferred, but not required.

PHYSICAL REQUIREMENTS	RARELY (0–12%)	OCCASIONALLY (12–33%)	FREQUENTLY (34–66%)	REGULARLY (67–100%)
Seeing: Must be able to read reports and use computer.				X
Hearing: Must be able to hear well enough to communicate with co-workers.				X
Standing/Walking	X			
Climbing/Stooping/Kneeling:	X			
Lifting/Pulling/Pushing:	X			
Fingering/Grasping/Feeling: Must be able to write, type, and use phone system.				X

Working Conditions: Normal working conditions with the absence of disagreeable elements.

Note: The statements herein are intended to describe the general nature and level of work being performed by employees, and are not to be construed as an exhaustive list of responsibilities, duties, and skills required of personnel so classified. Furthermore, they do not establish a contract for employment and are subject to change at the discretion of the employer.

Glossary

4/5ths rule when the selection rate for any protected group is less than 80% (4/5) of the selection rate for the majority group or less than 80% of the group's representation in the relevant labor market, discrimination exists.

401(k) plan an agreement in which a percentage of an employee's pay is withheld and invested in a tax-deferred account.

A

ability tests assess the skills that individuals have already learned.

active practice when trainees perform job-related tasks and duties during training.

affirmative action occurs when employers identify problem areas, set goals, and take positive steps to guarantee equal employment opportunities for people in a protected class.

applicant pool all people who are actually evaluated for selection.

applicant population a subset of the labor force population that is available for selection using a particular recruiting approach.

aptitude tests measure general ability to learn or acquire a skill.

arbitration a process that uses a neutral third party to make a decision.

attitude survey focuses on employees' feelings and beliefs about their jobs and the organization.

B

balance-sheet approach a program that provides international employees with a compensation package that equalizes cost differences between the international assignment and the same assignment in the home country of the individual or the corporation.

bargaining unit composed of all employees eligible to select a single union to represent and bargain collectively for them.

base pay the basic compensation that an employee receives, usually as a wage or salary.

behavior modeling copying someone else's behavior—the most elementary way in which people learn.

behavioral description interview applicants are required to give specific examples of how they have performed a certain procedure or handled a problem in the past.

behaviorally experienced training training efforts that focus less on physical skills than on attitudes, perceptions, and interpersonal issues.

benchmark jobs jobs that are found in many other organizations and are performed by several individuals who have similar duties that are relatively stable and that require similar knowledge, skills, and abilities.

benchmark measures training evaluation measures that are compared from one organization to others.

benchmarking a method of assessing HR effectiveness by comparing specific measures of performance against data on those measures in other "best practices" organizations.

benefit an indirect reward, such as health insurance, vacation pay, or retirement pensions, given to an employee or group of employees as a part of organizational membership.

bonus a one-time compensation payment that does not become part of the employee's base pay.

broadbanding a compensation plan that uses fewer pay grades having broader ranges than traditional compensation systems.

C

central tendency error occurs when appraisers rate all employees within a narrow range (usually the middle or average).

closed shop requires individuals to join a union before they can be hired.

co-determination a common practice in European countries that requires firms to have union or worker representatives on their boards of directors.

collective bargaining process whereby representatives of management and workers negotiate over wages, hours, and other terms and conditions of employment.

commission an individual incentive plan in which compensation is computed as a percentage of sales in units or dollars.

compa-ratio the pay level divided by the midpoint of the pay range; used to base pay adjustments.

compensable factor factor used to identify a job value that is commonly present throughout a group of jobs.

compensation committee a subgroup of the board of directors composed of directors who are not officers of the firm; generally makes recommendations to the board of directors on overall pay policies, salaries for top officers, supplemental compensation such as stock options and bonuses, and additional perks for executives.

compensatory time off given in lieu of payment for extra time worked, often called comp time.

competencies basic characteristics that can be linked to enhanced performance by individuals or teams of individuals.

complaint an indication of employee dissatisfaction that has not been submitted in writing; an outlet for hidden dissatisfaction.

conciliation when a third part attempts to keep union and management negotiators talking so that they can reach a voluntary settlement but makes no proposals for solutions.

concurrent validity a test is given to current employees and scores are correlated with their job performance. High correlation suggests that the test discriminates between employees with good and poor performance records.

construct validity shows a relationship between an abstract characteristic, or *construct,* inferred from research and job performance. Motivation and learning are examples of psychological constructs.

content validity a logical, nonstatistical method used to identify the knowledge, skills, and abilities (KSAs) and other characteristics necessary to perform a job.

contractual rights rights based on a specific contractual agreement with an employer.

culture the societal forces affecting the values, beliefs, and actions of a distinct group of people.

cumulative trauma disorders (CTDs) occur when workers repetitively use the same muscles to perform tasks, resulting in muscle and skeletal injuries.

D

decertification an election process used by employees who have a union and no longer wish to be represented by it.

development growing capabilities that go beyond those required by the current job; represent efforts to improve employees' abilities to handle a variety of assignments.

discipline a form of training that enforces organizational rules.

disparate impact occurs when there is substantial underrepresentation of protected-class members as a result of employment decisions that work to their disadvantage.

disparate treatment occurs when protected-class members are treated differently from others.

distributive justice the perceived fairness of the amounts given for performance; how pay relates to performance.

downsizing reducing the size of an organizational workforce.

due process the opportunity for individuals to explain and defend their actions against charges of misconduct or other reasons.

dues checkoff a union security provision that provides that union dues will be deducted automatically from the payroll checks of union members.

duty a larger work segment composed of several tasks that are performed by an individual.

E

employee assistance program (EAP) program that provides counseling and other help to employees having emotional, physical, or other personal problems.

employee benefits indirect compensation, such as pensions, health insurance, time off with pay, and so on.

employee stock ownership plan (ESOP) a type of profit sharing designed to give employees stock ownership of the organization for which they work, thereby increasing their commitment, loyalty, and effort.

employment-at-will (EAW) a common-law doctrine stating that employers have the right to hire, fire, demote, or promote whomever they choose, unless there is a law or contract to the contrary.

entitlement philosophy a compensation philosophy that traditionally gives automatic increases to employees each year, regardless of changing industry or economic conditions.

environmental scanning the process of studying the environment of the organization to pinpoint opportunities and threats.

equal employment opportunity (EEO) a broad concept holding that individuals should have equal treatment in all employment-related actions.

ergonomics the proper design of the work environment to address the physical demands experienced by people.

essential job functions functions necessary to perform the job; spelled out in written job descriptions indicating the time required to perform them and how critical they are.

exempt employees who hold positions classified as executive, administrative, professional, or outside sales, to whom employers are not required to pay overtime.

exit interview when those who are leaving the organization are asked to identify the reasons for their departure.

expatriate an employee working in a unit or plant who is not a citizen of the country in which the unit or plant is located but is a citizen of the country in which the organization is headquartered.

F

federation a group of autonomous national and international unions.

flexible spending accounts allows employees to contribute pretax dollars to buy additional benefits.

forced distribution a technique for distributing ratings that can be generated with any of the other methods.

forecasting using information from the past and present to identify expected future conditions.

G

gainsharing sharing greater-than-expected gains in profits and/or productivity with employees.

glass ceiling discriminatory practices that have prevented women and protected-class members from advancing to executive-level jobs.

global organization an enterprise that has corporate units in a number of countries that are integrated to operate as one organization worldwide.

golden parachute a special perk that provides protection and security to executives in the event that they lose their jobs or their firms are acquired by other firms.

graphic rating scale allows the rater to mark an employee's performance on a continuum.

green-circled employee an individual who is paid below the range set for the job.

grievance a complaint that has been put in writing and thus made formal.

grievance arbitration a means by which disputes arising from different interpretations of a labor contract are settle by a third party.

grievance procedures formal communications channels designed to settle a grievance as soon as possible after the problem arises.

H

halo effect occurs when a manager rates an employee high or low on all items because of one characteristic.

health refers to a general state of physical, mental, and emotional well-being.

health maintenance organization (HMO) a type of managed-care plan that provides services for a fixed period on a prepaid basis.

host-country national an employee working in a unit or plant who is a citizen of the country in which the unit or plant is located, when the unit or plant is operated by an organization headquartered in another country.

HR strategies the means used to aid the organization in managing the supply and demand for human resources.

human resource (HR) management deals with the design of formal systems in an organization to ensure the effective and efficient use of human talent to accomplish organizational goals.

human resource (HR) planning the process of analyzing and identifying the need for and availability of human resources.

human resource information system (HRIS) an integrated system designed to provide information used in HR decision making.

I

immediate confirmation learning concept that shows that people learn best if reinforcement is given soon after training.

importing and exporting the first phase of international interaction whereby an organization begins selling to and buying goods and services from organizations in other countries.

individual incentives given to reward the effort and performance of individuals (piece-rate systems, sales commissions, and bonuses).

individual-centered career planning focuses on individual's careers rather than on organizational needs.

J

job a grouping of common tasks, duties, and responsibilities.

job analysis a systematic way to gather and analyze information about the content and human requirement of jobs, and the context in which jobs are performed.

job criteria job performance dimensions that identify the elements most important in a job.

job description indicates the tasks, duties, and responsibilities of a job; identifies what is done, why it is done, where it is done, and how it is done.

job evaluation provides a systematic basis for determining the relative worth of jobs within an organization.

job family a grouping of jobs with similar characteristics.

job posting and bidding a means of recruiting employees for other jobs within the organization whereby employers provide notices of job openings and employees respond by applying for specific openings.

job responsibilities obligations to perform certain tasks and duties.

job rotation a widely used development technique whereby an employee spends time in different departments, fostering a greater understanding of the organization.

job specifications list the knowledge, skills, and abilities (KSAs) an individual needs to perform a job satisfactorily.

just cause sufficient justification for employment-related actions such as dismissal.

L

labor force population all individuals who are available for selection if all possible recruitment strategies are used.

labor markets external sources from which employers attract employees.

learning a psychological construct.

local unions may be centered on a particular employer organization or around a particular geographic location.

lockout when management shuts down company operations to prevent union members from working.

lump-sum increase (LSI) a one-time payment of all or part of a yearly pay increase.

M

managed care consists of approaches that monitor and reduce medical costs using restrictions and market system alternatives.

management by objectives (MBO) the performance goals that an individual hopes to attain within an appropriate length of time.

management rights provisions rights reserved to the employer to manage, direct, and control its business.

market line a line showing the relationship between job value, as determined by job evaluation points, and pay survey rates.

market price the typical wage paid for a job in the immediate labor market.

massed practice when a person does all of the practice on job-related tasks at once.

mediation when a third party assists the negotiators in their discussions and also suggests settlement proposals.

mental ability tests measure reasoning capabilities.

mentoring a relationship in which managers at the midpoints in their careers aid individuals in the earlier stages of their careers.

multinational enterprise (MNE) an enterprise in which organizational units are located in foreign countries.

N

national emergency strike one that would affect an industry or a major part of it such that the national economy would be significantly affected.

national unions and international unions unions not governed by the federation even if they are affiliated with it.

nonexempt employees who must be paid overtime under the Fair Labor Standards Act.

O

organization chart depicts the relationships among jobs in an organization.

organization incentives rewards people for the performance of the entire organization.

organizational commitment the degree to which employees believe in and accept organizational goals and want to remain with the organization.

organization-centered career planning efforts focusing on constructing career paths that provide for the logical progression of people between jobs in an organization.

orientation the planned introduction of new employees to their jobs, their co-workers, and the organization.

outplacement a group of services provided to displaced employees to give them support and assistance.

P

panel interview several interviewers who interview a candidate at the same time.

pay compression occurs when the range of pay differences among individuals with different levels of experience and performance becomes small.

pay equity the concept that the pay for all jobs requiring comparable knowledge, skills, and abilities should be similar even if actual duties and market rates differ significantly.

pay grades used to group individual jobs having approximately the same job worth in the process of establishing pay structures.

peer review panel composed of employees who hear appeals from disciplined employees and make recommendations of decisions.

pension plans retirement benefits established and funded by employers and employees.

performance appraisal the process of evaluating how well employees perform their jobs when compared to a set of standards, and then communicating that information to those employees.

performance management system the processes used to identify, encourage, measure, evaluate, improve, and reward employee performance at work.

performance philosophy a compensation philosophy in which no one is guaranteed increased compensation by adding another year of organizational service; instead, pay and incentives are based on performance differences among employees.

performance standards flow directly from a job description, telling what the job accomplishes and how performance is measured in key areas of the job description.

perquisites (perks) special executive benefits-usually noncash items such as private club memberships or first class air travel privileges.

piece-rate system an individual incentive plan in which compensation is computed on a per piece rate based on predetermined standards.

placement fitting a person to the right job.

policies general guidelines that focus organizational actions.

position a job performed by one person.

predictive validity test results of applicants are compared with their subsequent job performance.

predictors identifiable indicators of the selection criteria.

preferred provider organization (PPO) a type of managed-care plan whereby a health-care provider contracts with an employer or an employer group to provide health-care services to employees at a competitive rate.

procedural justice the perceived fairness of the process and procedures used to make decisions about employees, including their pay.

procedures customary methods of handling activities; more specific than policies.

productivity a measure of the quantity and quality of work done, considering the cost of the resources it took to do the work.

profit sharing distributing some portion of organizational profits to employees.

protected class those sharing certain designated characteristics, such as race, age, or gender, who are protected by law from discrimination in employment.

psychological contract the unwritten expectations that employees and employers have about the nature of their work relationships.

R

ranking a method of listing all employees from highest to lowest in performance.

rater bias occurs when a rater's values or prejudices distort the rating.

realistic job preview (RJP) informs job candidates of the "organizational realities" of a job so they can more accurately evaluate their own job expectations.

red-circled employee an incumbent who is paid above the range set for the job.

reengineering rethinking and redesigning work to improve cost, service, and speed.

reinforcement concept based on the *law of effect*, which states that people tend to repeat responses that give them some type of positive reward and avoid actions associated with negative consequences.

reliability the consistency with which a test measures an item.

repatriation the process of bringing expatriates home.

replacement charts part of the development planning process specifying the nature of development each employee needs in order to be prepared for the identified promotions.

reverse discrimination exists when a person is denied an opportunity because of preferences given to a member of a protected class who may be less qualified.

right to privacy freedom from unauthorized and unreasonable intrusion into their personal affairs.

rules specific guidelines that regulate and restrict the behavior of individuals.

S

safety refers to protecting the physical well-being of people.

security protection of employer facilities and equipment from unauthorized access and protection of employees while they are on work premises or work assignments.

security audit a comprehensive analysis of the vulnerability of organizational security.

selection the process of choosing qualified individuals to fill jobs in an organization.

selection criterion a characteristic that a person must have to do a job successfully.

selection interview designed to identify information on a candidate and clarify information from other sources.

self-directed work team composed of individuals who are assigned a cluster of tasks, duties, and responsibilities to be accomplished.

seniority time spent in the organization or on a particular job; can be used as the basis for pay increases.

severance pay a security benefit voluntarily offered by employers to employees who lose their jobs.

spaced practice when training practice sessions on job-related tasks are spaced over a period of hours or days.

stock option the right to buy stock in a company, usually at an advantageous price.

strike when union members refuse to work in order to put pressure on an employer.

structured interview a set of standardized questions that are asked of all applicants so that comparisons among applicants can more easily be made.

substance abuse the use of illicit substances or the misuse of controlled substances, alcohol, or other drugs.

T

task a distinct, identifiable work activity composed of motions.

tax equalization plan a plan in which the company adjusts an employee's base income downward by the amount of estimated U.S. tax to be paid for the year, ensuring that expatriates pay no more or less than if they had stayed in the United States.

team or group incentives when an entire group is rewarded for its performance; most commonly used are gainsharing plans, in which employee teams or groups that meet certain goals share in the gains measured against performance targets.

temporary employees temporary workers hired on a rate-per-day or per-week basis.

third-country national a citizen of one country, working in a second country, and employed by an organization headquartered in a third country.

turnover occurs when employees leave an organization and have to be replaced.

U

undue hardship an action that imposes significant difficulty or expense on an employer.

unemployment compensation provides benefits to people who lose their jobs; required by law, but provisions vary from state to state.

union a formal association of workers that promotes the interests of its members through collective action.

union authorization card card signed by an employee to designate a union as his or her collective bargaining agent.

union security provisions contract provisions to aid the union in obtaining and retaining members.

V

validity the extent to which a test actually measures what it says it measures.

variable pay compensation linked directly to performance accomplishments, such as bonuses and incentive program payments.

variable pay compensation linked to individual, team, and/or organization performance.

variable pay plans plans established that focus on individual performance, team or group performance, and organization-wide performance; these incentives may increase the degree of cooperation in teams, whereas individual incentives do not.

W

wage and salary administration the development, implementation, and ongoing maintenance of a base pay system.

wages payment made to employees who are paid hourly, directly calculated on the amount of time worked.

wellness programs programs to encourage self-directed lifestyle changes.

whistle-blowers individuals who report real or perceived wrongs committed by their employers.

work analysis studies the workflow, activities, context, and output of a job.

workers' compensation provides benefits to people injured on the job; required by law.

wrongful discharge occurs when an employer terminates an individual's employment for reasons that are illegal or improper.

Index

A

Absenteeism, employees', 23
Academy of Management, 177
Accidents. *See* Injuries
Accommodation for disabled individuals, 46–47
Active practice, defined, 78
Affirmative action plan, 5
    defined, 39
    equal employment opportunity and, 39–40
    reverse discrimination and, 40
    who must have, 42
AFL. *See* American Federation of Labor
AFL-CIO, 177
Age discrimination, 45–46
Aging population, health-care jobs and, 2, 3
American Arbitration Association, 177
American Federation of Labor, 157
American Management Association, 177
American Payroll Association, 177
American Society for Industrial Security, 177
American Society for Public Administration, 177
American Society for Training and Development, 177
American Society of Safety Engineers, 177
American Staffing Association, 177
Americans with Disabilities Act, 37, 46
    job analysis and, 54
    job description and, 59
    medical examinations and, 73
    substance abuse issues and, 143
    workers' compensation issues and, 137
Applicant pool, defined, 62
Applicant population, defined, 61
Application forms
    purpose of, 69–70
    weighted, 70–71
Aptitude tests, 71
Arbitration
    defined, 163
    grievance, 166
Assignments, international
    selection for, 29–30
    training and development for, 30–31
Association of Executive Search Consultants, 177
Attitude survey, defined, 25
Attrition, defined, 14

B

Balance-sheet approach, defined, 31
Bargaining unit, defined, 160
Base pay, defined, 104
Behavior modeling, defined, 78
Behavioral description interview, defined, 73
Behavioral/objectives methods, performance appraisal through, 99–100
Behaviorally experienced training, 81
Benchmark jobs, 112
Benchmark measures, 82
Benchmarking, defined, 25
Benefits
    administration, 132–133
    classified by type, 128
    defined, 104
    health-care, 129–131